VISION AND DISCERNMENT

VISION AND DISCERNMENT:
An Orientation in Theological Study

Charles M. Wood

Wipf and Stock Publishers
150 West Broadway • Eugene OR 97401

Wipf and Stock Publishers
150 West Broadway
Eugene, Oregon 97401

Vision and Discernment
An Orientation in Theological Study
By Wood, Charles M.
©1985 Wood, Charles M.
ISBN: 1-57910-870-9
Publication date: January, 2002
Previously published by Scholars Press, 1985.

CONTENTS

Preface

This book offers an orientation in Christian theology, broadly conceived. Its subject is not that single discipline in the theological curriculum to which the title of "theology" is nowadays often reserved, i.e., systematic theology or dogmatics, but rather the whole curriculum, or the whole range of disciplines which together constitute the enterprise of Christian theology, and whose study constitutes theological education.

The possibility of such a comprehensive orientation has appeared increasingly remote over the past several decades. It has become very difficult to think of theology as a whole—that is, to think of the collection of studies in a theological curriculum as having any internal unity, or, for that matter, any common aim. Courses in "theological encyclopedia"— the old name for an orientation to theological studies in their unity and variety—disappeared from most seminary curricula by early in this century, along with their textbooks; meanwhile the term "theology" dropped out of the titles of more and more courses and curricular divisions apart from the area of "systematic theology" (which had already long been regarded as "theology" *par excellence,* and was now, in effect, given exclusive rights to the title); and the study and teaching of the Bible, of church history, of ethics, of "theology," of the functions of ministry, and of various attendant disciplines have since proceeded more or less along their own tracks, often making very little difference to one another.

In some ways, of course, this has been a healthy development—simply a continuation of the process begun over two centuries ago when these studies began to come out from under dogmatic and ecclesiastical control, and to develop into independent, critical disciplines. The enormously productive modern revolutions in biblical studies, church history, the study of religions, pastoral care, and other fields would not have been possible if these had not become, in a sense, non-theological studies. It was necessary for them to cast off the constraints of inherited theological decisions concerning their subject-matter and concerning the methods of study appropriate to it, and to adopt instead the resources of such emerging "secular" disciplines as critical history, anthropology, and sociology, in order to make the breakthroughs in method and substance which have given us our present understandings of these areas. In *that* sense, they had to become non-theological, even secular, disciplines themselves. In a sense to be explored in this book, this secularization has given them the potential to become truly theological disciplines.

But it has also made their theological utility less obvious, and perhaps more difficult to specify. An analogy may be helpful: A citizen who is critical of the government's policies may appear less patriotic than a jingoist who simply identifies loyalty to those policies with loyalty to country. The critical citizen's words and actions may at times be indistinguishable from those of avowed enemies of the nation, even though they may express a truer and a more effective loyalty than the jingoist's uncritical support. The critic's patriotism is, perhaps, less obvious than the flag-waving variety. It may involve raising some searching questions not only about particular government policies or practices, but about such things as national purpose, the meaning of citizenship and patriotism, and the relationship of national loyalty to other loyalties. It may involve trying to see one's nation from the outside as well as the inside, seeking to correct the distortions which self-interest imposes upon perception. There is nothing necessarily patriotic about such a probing inquiry. Others can raise the same questions, from other motives. Explaining how this sort of inquiry is not only compatible with but at times demanded by responsible citizenship can be a complex task, particularly when a simpler view of what loyalty requires would suggest that such questioning amounts to disloyalty, or at least must inevitably lead to an erosion of one's allegiance.

Just so, the task of explaining how the various critical inquiries which reside in the contemporary theological curriculum are, or at any rate could be, ordered to a genuine theological purpose and contribute to one coherent process of reflection in the service of the church is not a simple one. It means asking what Christian theology really is, as well as what distinguishes and unifies its components as theological disciplines. The task is further complicated by the fact that there has been little consensus, either within or among the disciplines involved, as to how these questions should be answered, and that this lack of consensus is reflected in (among other things) a certain incoherence in the typical theological curriculum. The renunciation of an earlier, imposed consensus may have enabled these disciplines to gain their critical independence and, with it, the promise of becoming "truly theological" in a more profound sense. But that more profound sense has yet to be clearly and effectively articulated or decisively embodied in the actual structures and procedures of theological study and instruction. This means that any current attempt at orientation in Christian theology must take the form of a proposal, embodying at least an implicit critique of the arrangements typically encountered in contemporary theological education.

Such a proposal may have several uses, particularly to two groups of people: In the first place, it may help those who are entering upon the study of theology to envision that study as a whole—to reflect upon the relationships among its parts, and to put things together in their own minds. It may help them to raise questions which would not otherwise occur, to see connections among different areas of study, and to develop some useful patterns of reflection and habits of inquiry. In short, it may assist them to set about the task of acquiring a theological education with the resources at hand. Secondly, such a proposal may be useful to those engaged at a more advanced level in theological scholarship and theological education, for many of the same reasons. It may stimulate some useful lines of reflection on the nature of a particular discipline, or on the relationships among disciplines, or on the purposes of a theological school, or on theological teaching. It might suggest some possibilities for revision or reform in one or another of these areas. For neither group, of course, is the proposal's usefulness contingent upon its being found entirely convincing; even an outrageous proposal can be useful, if it manages somehow to generate and nourish thinking. The proposal set forth in this book does not aim to be outrageous—a fact which, of course, carries no guarantee.

The book has five chapters. The first ventures a brief sketch of the recent history and current situation of theological study, and relates the task of the book to that context. The second chapter then offers a definition of Christian theology, and unfolds some of its implications. The third develops that definition further, giving an account of the essential structure of theological inquiry. The fourth chapter turns to a consideration of the dynamics of that inquiry, and proposes a distinctive understanding of systematic theology as a process of reflection involving complementary activities of judgment identified as "vision" and "discernment." In the fifth chapter, finally, theological education is depicted as the enterprise of developing a capacity and disposition for theological inquiry, and this depiction of it is related to some other influential accounts of its mission. In each of these chapters, the focus is kept on the essential lines of the positive proposal being developed. Although the argument requires some attention to the history of theological study, and to alternative proposals, older and recent, the amount of historical interpretation and of critical engagement with alternatives has been kept to a minimum. To do justice either to this history or to those alternatives would require quite a different sort of book, which would not as readily serve the uses for which this one is intended.

My indebtedness to others who have written about these issues will be obvious. Specific debts, insofar as I am conscious of them, are acknowledged in the text and notes. This preface is the appropriate place to acknowledge other sorts of help. I am grateful to Perkins School of Theology, Southern Methodist University, for the provision of a year's research leave during which the greater part of the work on this book was done; but beyond that, I am happy to record my gratitude for the continuing stimulus and support of a lively community of theological inquiry which that school sustains. The Association of Theological Schools has supplied through its Issues Research Program both a research grant and the opportunity for consultation with other participants similarly engaged in studies pertinent to theological education. I thank the Association's executive director, Dr. Leon Pacala, his staff, and my colleagues in that program for their assistance and encouragement.

I am particularly thankful to Professor James O. Duke and Professor Schubert M. Ogden for their comments upon the manuscript, which have helped me to clarify and strengthen it in certain respects.

An earlier version of the third chapter of this book appeared under the title, "An Orientation in Christian Theology," in *Encounter*, 45, 3 (Summer 1984). I have also incorporated into the same chapter some material from my chapter, "Wesleyan Constructive Theology?" in *Wesleyan Theology Today*, edited by Theodore Runyon (Nashville: The United Methodist Publishing House, 1985), which had earlier appeared as an article under the same title in the *Perkins Journal*, 37, 3 (Spring 1984). A slightly edited version of Chapter Five appeared in *Theological Education*, 21, 2 (Spring 1985).

C.M.W.

Chapter I
Toward Understanding Our Context

When Friedrich Schleiermacher completed the manuscript of his *Brief Outline on the Study of Theology* in December of 1811, he wrote his friend Joachim Christian Gass that he was curious as to what its readers would find in it. He wondered whether they would think it heretical. He suspected (he said) that they would at least declare it to be full of ghosts—"theological disciplines which have never existed and never will."[1] The scheme he was setting forth in the *Brief Outline* had become so familiar to Schleiermacher himself, both as a guide to his own thinking and as the outline of his standard course in "theological encyclopedia," that it seemed quite proper and natural. Yet he was aware that it was a highly individual, constructive vision of the nature and organization of theology, something quite different from the way theological study as a whole had been previously conceived. It was his recognition of a crisis in theological study, brought on by the growing conflict between traditional models of theology and theological education on the one hand and modern methods of inquiry and the modern context of theology on the other, which had led Schleiermacher to develop his own innovative proposal as to how that study might be coherently envisioned and pursued.

That crisis had its origins in the seventeenth century, but had grown increasingly acute during the eighteenth. The Protestant reformers and their theological successors had devised various schemes for organizing the study of theology in ways that would serve the needs of the Protestant movement, chiefly by preparing pastors and teachers who were competent to guide and defend the churches. The fundamental task was, of course, the study of the Bible; theology was to be rooted in—indeed, for some it was simply identical with—biblical exegesis, centering on the biblical witness as the source and standard of Christian faith and life. But there were other tasks, branching from this exegetical trunk. Although there was much deliberate opposition to the scholastic tradition of Roman Catholic theology (in which, it was thought, Aristotle had supplanted scripture and knowledge was exalted over faith), the need

---

[1]Quoted by Heinrich Scholz in his introduction to Friedrich Schleiermacher, *Kurze Darstellung des theologischen Studiums zum Behuf einleitender Vorlesungen*, ed. Heinrich Scholz (Hildesheim: Georg Olms, 1961), xvii.

for some way of arranging biblical teaching into a coherent presentation of Christian doctrine was generally recognized; and thus the curriculum normally included a branch devoted to this effort, known variously as "dogmatic" or "acroamatic" or (occasionally) "systematic" theology. Whatever the title, the choice of method for such a presentation of doctrine was ordinarily dictated by what was thought to be pedagogical effectiveness, in view of both the nature of the subject and the needs of the students. The typical course of studies also featured the study of church history and the history of doctrine, with an eye toward the vindication of the Protestant movement against Roman Catholic claims. This study, too, was governed by the principle of "scripture alone," in two important ways: First, because "tradition" was not to be regarded as authoritative in its own right, but only insofar as it is commensurate with scripture, the study of church history was conceived as a critical examination of tradition, pursuing the question of its faithfulness to its scriptural charter. The spirit of such works as Martin Luther's treatise on *The Babylonian Captivity of the Church* informed this study, and, although there were pre-Reformation examples of it, this sort of critical approach was taken to be distinctively Protestant. Second, as the title of Luther's treatise itself suggests, scripture offered to this study more than a principle of criticism. It offered abundant resources for the understanding of the church's history and present state, ranging from piecemeal insights into the human condition and illuminating historical analogies all the way to comprehensive visions of the course of world history from creation to consummation, within which the real significance of specific events of post-scriptural history (e.g., the rise of the Papacy, the Muslim invasion of Europe) could be grasped. The Protestant study of church history thus typically combined a critical examination of tradition with some sort of theological interpretation of history, in which the providential role of the Reformation itself was ordinarily given particular attention.

The fourth major area of study (in addition to the biblical, dogmatic, and historical) was the pastoral office itself. Like the other three areas, this one demanded a new beginning in the Protestant setting; although certain patterns of thought and conceptual categories were carried forward from the Roman Catholic legacy in this area too, the Protestant conception of the pastoral office (as well as of the Bible, of the church's historical career, and of the task of dogmatics) set a new theological agenda. Here, too, as with the other two subordinate branches, scripture was taken to be normative, and the task was seen as one of translating scriptural patterns of church leadership and scriptural wisdom concerning its exercise into the contemporary setting.[2]

---

[2] See Carl Friedrich Stäudlin, *Geschichte der theologischen Wissenschaften seit der Verbreitung der alten Litteratur*, I (Göttingen: Vandenhoek und Ruprecht, 1810), 138–43. This work of a

The fourfold pattern of theological studies—biblical, dogmatic/systematic, historical, and practical—which has dominated curricular organization into our own day thus had its origins in the Reformation, and more specifically in the effort to equip Protestant pastors and teachers with certain requisite knowledge, abilities, and understandings. The persistence of this pattern ever since, despite the many ways in which both theological studies and church leadership have changed over the years, is attributable in part to the power of a common perception that its divisions still represent what the church's leaders need. (This is not to deny the contributions of a variety of other factors, social and political as well as intellectual, which are themselves interwoven with that perception.) The presence or absence of a more formal rationale for the pattern—e.g., a demonstration that theology as such requires these four elements, no more and no less—has never been a major factor in its popularity, although such explanations have occasionally been attempted. Instead, the greatest challenges to the pattern and to certain of its constituent elements have been on its own practical terms: Is this what ministers really need? Even if this approach once served us well, is it still the way we ought to prepare persons for church leadership? Such questions were raised by some already in the eighteenth century, and have been pressed with increasing frequency and urgency in more recent times, for at least two major reasons.

First, as the four components of the pattern have developed their own independent identities as scholarly disciplines, their pertinence to the preparation of church leaders has sometimes come into question. Although the fourfold *pattern* has persisted, the character of each of its components has changed markedly, so that the relationship of these disciplines to the old purposes is not always clear. How, for example, is the critical historical study of the Bible supposed to equip a pastor to understand and proclaim its message as the "Word of God," the criterion for Christian existence? Or what does the study of church history, understood now neither as a polemical exercise against Rome nor as the story of God's providential activity but rather as a critical investigation of the life and thought of various human communities in the past, have to do with pastoral responsibilities in our vastly different present? Or, what's the use of whatever presently goes by the name of "systematic theology"?

Secondly, even if the fourfold pattern were still serving its old purposes, conceptions of church leadership have changed. The adequacy

---

contemporary of Schleiermacher is still illuminating in its perspective and detail. Two much more recent useful accounts of the history and literature of theological study are those of Wolfhart Pannenberg, *Theology and the Philosophy of Science,* tr. Francis McDonagh (Philadelphia: Westminster Press, 1976), especially chs. 4 and 6, and Edward Farley, *Theologia: The Fragmentation and Unity of Theological Education* (Philadelphia: Fortress Press, 1983).

for the contemporary church of an educational scheme designed essentially to serve the needs of the sixteenth-century pastor and congregation is at least debatable. As the notion, practice, and context of church leadership have changed, the fourfold pattern has more and more seemed not merely insufficient so far as its traditional content is concerned but also inappropriate in its very structure. It has seemed reasonable to ask not only whether we might not do well to substitute some new ingredients for some old ones (for instance, a little more training in conflict management, a little less church history), but also whether a thorough transformation of the whole structure of theological education is not in order. Some of the more influential proposals for the revision of American theological education in recent decades have taken this route. Starting with an empirically-informed description of the current role and functions of the Protestant ministry, they have asked how education for ministry ought to be conceived so as to be effective preparation for that actual ministry. However, the general impact of these proposals has not been to dislodge the fourfold pattern, but rather to increase the proportion of curricular time devoted to an increasingly specialized set of "practical" studies, often supplemented by field education or internship, and to encourage a view of the other three areas as constituting the "theoretical" portion of the curriculum.[3] This in turn has increased the pressure on these "theoretical" areas to justify their own relevance to ministerial education. At the same time, the growing emphasis on and specialization of the practical studies creates pressure there as well: students often find themselves introduced to a series of disciplines, mostly centered in discrete pastoral functions, each with its own literature and history. Often they lack time and opportunity to get beneath the surface of any of these, or to achieve any sense of coherence among them. There is a pervasive bewilderment not only as to the relationship between the "theoretical" and "practical" divisions of the curriculum, but also as to the relationships of the practical studies—each with its own theoretical orientation—to each other and to the practice of ministry.

When the fourfold pattern was first established, each of its four components was so conceived and pursued as to have an immediate relevance to the needs of church leadership. Biblical study not only helped to form the student's faith, understanding, and character as a Christian, but also taught the skills of theological exegesis needed to open the Word of God to the congregation. Dogmatic theology was a way of getting hold of what was taken to be the doctrinal content of scripture so that its

[3] See Robert Wood Lynn, "Notes Toward a History: Theological Encyclopedia and the Evolution of Protestant Seminary Curriculum, 1808–1968," *Theological Education*, 17 (1981), 118–144.

coherence and rationality were visible to the mind, and so that it could be readily remembered and appropriately conveyed in situations of teaching or controversy. Historical study served, it was thought, to orient the student to the present context, not only in the course of tradition but in the pattern of God's providence, so that the resources of the past could be intelligently appropriated. The study of the pastoral office equipped the student with an understanding of its nature and duties and, to some extent, with the skills to function therein—though pastoral formation was understood to be, and was, the product of the whole course of studies and of its context in a community of faith, and not merely the responsibility of one curricular area.

But in the course of the eighteenth century (with some anticipations earlier), fundamental changes occurred in each of these areas, and in the whole context of theological education. Both biblical and church-historical studies were transformed by the application to them of newly-developed critical historical methods. It is not that these theological disciplines were suddenly secularized; rather, several things occurred, gradually and more or less simultaneously, to transform them into an uneasy mixture of the old and the new. First, some probing questions were raised concerning the relationship between the way in which the subject-matter of these disciplines was theologically regarded and its scholarly investigation. For example, can one reconcile a view of the Bible as the "Word of God" with a treatment of it as the product of human experience and effort? Can one regard it as authoritative, and at the same time raise questions about the origin and validity of its content? Or again, what does a fully critical approach to church history require, and how does that square with the conventional theological interpretation of this history, or with the conventional use of categories such as "heresy" and "orthodoxy," or with the official understandings church bodies have of themselves and of each other? Secondly, the results of the new critical scholarship were powerfully impressive—not least in their undermining of many traditional claims in which theology appeared to have an interest (e.g., as to the authorship, composition, and historical reliability of various biblical writings). Critical historical study was bearing fruit, and the results carried conviction, often to the detriment of traditional beliefs. Thirdly, an acceptance of the newer scholarship was rapidly becoming a condition of theology's participation in the renewed universities, particularly in Germany, where the complex relationship between university, state, and church meant that theology had no real option but to face the challenges posed by modern secular studies. The "theological sciences" could accredit themselves as sciences (i.e., proper scholarly disciplines, productive of genuine knowledge) only by identifying themselves methodologically with their non-theological cognate disciplines and opening their subject matter to fully critical investigation.[4] This state of affairs naturally gave rise to the question of what any longer made these theological disciplines *theological,* and indeed of what constituted them as discrete disciplines at all. Why "biblical studies" rather than, say, ancient Near Eastern and Hellenistic history? Why "church history" rather than, say, European history, African history, etc., or the history of religions? The point is not just that the subject matter of these "theological" disciplines may be subsumed readily under one or more of the secular historical fields. It is also that (as scholars began to recognize) to treat "the Bible" or "the New Testament" or "the church" as a distinct subject matter is an historically dubious procedure, encouraging a misconstrual of the relationships of certain texts and events to each other and a slighting of their actual historical contexts.

As the biblical and historical branches of theological study were thus struggling for their identity in relation to historical science, dogmatic or systematic theology was undergoing its own transformation. Briefly, what happened was this: as the modern worldview began to emerge from its seventeenth-century beginnings, and to supplant the traditional, biblically-oriented worldview more and more, it fell to this branch of theological work to attempt that intellectual reconciliation of Christianity and the modern world which has occupied so large a part of the theological agenda ever since. Dogmatics was already understood as having the task of displaying the logical structure and intelligibility of the content of Christian faith—of bringing the faith somehow to reflective consciousness, making it rationally accessible; so this new assignment could be understood simply as an extension of its traditional role, even though it meant vast changes in dogmatic method and in theology as a whole. As before, philosophy played an important part: the work of particular philosophers—their concepts, categories, and arguments— continued to be appropriated for theological construction, while the term "philosophy" itself often continued to stand as a collective term for the activities and products of human intelligence, i.e., for the sum of secular knowledge, or for the prevalent general understanding of things with which the Christian faith had somehow to engage. But whereas earlier this engagement often meant incorporating elements of philosophy more or less coherently into the Christian framework, now it increasingly took the form of a thoroughgoing attempt to interpret and vindicate Christian belief in terms of one or another philosophical worldview. Given the vast changes in the perception of history and nature brought about by modern studies and discoveries, it was the

---

[4] For a compact statement of the problem, see Eberhard Jüngel, "Das Verhältnis der theologischen Disziplinen untereinander," *Unterwegs zur Sache: Theologische Bemerkungen* (Munich: Chr. Kaiser, ʾ972), 36–43.

philosophical scheme responsive to these changes, rather than the traditional biblical-classical synthesis, which was taken as the primary representation of reality. The historian Emanuel Hirsch summarizes the change memorably, if overdramatically, when he says that with the rise to prominence of the popular philosophy of Christian Wolff (1679–1754), philosophy ceased to be the servant of theology and became its ruler instead.[5] It is at least clear that the burden of proof was shifting. It was by becoming something like a philosophical account of the Christian faith that dogmatic theology assumed that burden, and simultaneously sought to justify its place in the university. Biblical and historical theology (or their successors) justified their standing in the university largely by focusing on the attainment of valid historical knowledge; systematic theology did so largely by centering on the question of the meaning and truth of Christian doctrine, i.e., by subjecting it to philosophical scrutiny and explication.

The fourth of the traditional areas of theological study, that dealing with ministerial practice, underwent less drastic change meanwhile. It was also less successful in establishing itself as a scholarly discipline, and retained a marginal status in the university—a status symbolized late in the eighteenth century by the treatment of pastoral theology in an appendix, rather than in the main text, of G. J. Planck's *Introduction to the Theological Sciences* (1794/95). Planck reasoned that because this area was concerned with the application rather than with the production of knowledge concerning religion, it did not belong among the genuine theological sciences.[6] The marginality of practical studies was further reinforced by the growing prestige in the universities of the ideal of *Wissenschaftlichkeit*, i.e., the disinterested pursuit of knowledge for its own sake, as contrasted with any sort of vocational training. The growth of this ideal, like the earlier emancipation of the universities from theological control, was due in part to an interest in unfettered inquiry, and in part to a desire to make and keep the universities attractive to a leisured aristocracy.[7] The cultivation and transmission of practical knowledge was left to other agencies and settings.

Not only was the field of practical theology as such regarded as "unscientific," but the other theological disciplines tended to lose their previous practicality as they gained scientific identity. The critical historical study of the Bible, for instance, brings the student into a different relationship to the text from that found in most precritical theological

---

[5] Emanuel Hirsch, *Geschichte der neuern evangelischen Theologie*, II (4th ed., Gütersloh: Gerd Mohn, 1951), 89.

[6] Walter Birnbaum, *Theologische Wandlungen von Schleiermacher bis Karl Barth* (Tübingen: Katzmann, 1963), 6–7.

[7] See Charles E. McClelland, *State, Society, and University in Germany, 1700–1914* (Cambridge: Cambridge University Press, 1980), 39–41, 118–125.

exegesis. Not only are different sorts of questions raised, but the inquiry as a whole is defined by a different aim. The consonance of critical historical study with the Protestant "scripture principle" was frequently asserted: clear away all the traditional theological assumptions and inter-pretations, and see what the text itself really says. But what a text "really says" depends in part on what one asks it, and the relationship between the historian's questions and those of a community for which the text is "scripture" is not always one of direct correspondence. The first inquiry may have some bearing upon the second, but cannot simply supplant it. Insofar as "biblical theology" was simply transformed into the critical historical study of the Bible, the problem of the right theological use of that study was both posed and ignored.

An analogous problem, though perhaps less severe, is raised by the critical study of church history, insofar as it involves the same sort of objective scrutiny of tradition, and raises questions about the claims of any church to represent what is normatively Christian, while leaving aside the question of how tradition is to be critically appropriated. In systematic theology, the transition from the essentially rhetorical ped-agogical style of, e.g., Philip Melanchthon's *Loci* of 1521 to the philosoph-ically-oriented systems of the eighteenth likewise meant a transition from an "engaged" mode of reflection on the substance of the Christian witness to a more speculative, or at any rate more narrowly intellectual, effort to render that witness intelligible. Assuming that the effort is successful, its relationship to the actual tasks of Christian proclamation, nurture, discipline, etc., or to the preparation of persons to engage effectively in these tasks, is still far from clear.

This, then, was the situation to which Schleiermacher addressed his proposal, and in terms of which the major features of that proposal can be most readily understood. Three of the four traditional branches of theological study had become full-fledged scholarly disciplines, so far as their essential aims and methodologies were concerned. They stressed the rigorous, critical pursuit of knowledge concerning their subject matter, utilizing the generally accepted scholarly procedures. Divisions and specializations within these disciplines had emerged. Scholars in each of the so-called theological disciplines were often finding that they had more in common with their fellow philologists, historians, or phi-losophers, elsewhere in the university, than with the representatives of the other theological disciplines. The transition from Latin to the ver-nacular as the language of theological discourse symbolized as well as facilitated the transformation of theology from a unified, tradition-oriented, churchly endeavor into a collection of modern critical studies.[8]

[8]Stäudlin, *Geschichte*, II (Göttingen: Vandenhoek und Ruprecht, 1811), 304.

Yet to the extent that this transformation was successful, it posed a fundamental question: What any longer constituted these disciplines as *theological* disciplines? What gave them their right to exist as disciplines distinct from the general historical and philosophical enterprises to which, in both method and material, they seemed to belong? What, if anything, identified and related them as the parts of a single study called "theology"? It sometimes appeared that the "theological sciences" could qualify as genuine *sciences* only by ceasing to be *theological*, i.e., by becoming indistinguishable from their cognate secular disciplines.[9] Meanwhile, the fourth branch of the traditional curriculum was retaining its theological identity—or so it seemed—only as a result of its virtual exclusion from the realm of scholarly investigation, and its continuing to function principally as the transmitter of traditional pastoral lore. This basic shift in the character and context of theological study, with all that it implies, gave Schleiermacher his agenda.

One of the major features of Schleiermacher's proposal signals his essentially positive response to this transformation and to the forces which impelled it—and particularly to the irreversible impact of critical historical consciousness upon theological reflection: his placement of a new discipline which he called *historical theology* at the center of theological study. It is the task of this discipline to furnish knowledge of the actual situation of the Christian church, past and present. Although the historical branch of the old fourfold scheme was sometimes designated "historical theology," Schleiermacher's discipline has a much broader scope as well as a clearer allegiance to the methods of secular historical study than its predecessor. It includes the study of the Bible, or what Schleiermacher called "exegetical theology": in his view, the old distinction between biblical and historical theology rested on a false conception of the uniqueness of the Bible, and is, moreover, out of keeping with the historical orientation of modern biblical scholarship. Schleiermacher therefore abolished it. Exegetical theology is simply that branch of historical theology which is concerned with the earliest and thus purest expressions of Christianity, those found in the New Testament; while "church history" (in which the history of dogma may be organized as a distinct subordinate study) is that branch concerned with its subsequent development to the present.

Besides exegetical theology and church history, historical theology also includes the study of the present situation of Christianity. Schleiermacher divides this study into two parts, one dealing with the social and institutional condition of the Christian community itself, and the other dealing with its ideas, its self-understanding. The first of these he calls "statistics"; the second, "dogmatics." With this latter move, another mem-

---

[9] See Jüngel, *loc. cit.*

ber of the traditional fourfold scheme has been subsumed under historical theology. Dogmatic theology is no longer understood as the orderly statement of Christian truth as such, or of the doctrinal content of the Bible, but rather as "the systematic presentation of doctrine now current in the Church."[10] It is, so to speak, the historical study of the leading edge of the development of Christian doctrine; but it is also a "systematic presentation" of this stage of development, i.e., of the church's current self-understanding—and this means it is a constructive effort to relate the orthodox and the heterodox, the traditional affirmations of creed and confession and the results of the church's more recent efforts to think through its faith anew in its present historical context.

Historical theology, thus broadened to include the material of the old-style biblical and dogmatic branches as well, forms "the actual corpus of theological study" in Schleiermacher's account.[11] However, theology is not simply historical study. If it were, its identity as theology would be lost, and it would have to be absorbed along with its subject matter, the Christian church, into the wider discipline of historical scholarship. Historical theology cannot stand alone as a discipline. The only justification for its peculiar focus upon the past and present condition of the Christian community is the fact that this focus serves another purpose than the attainment of knowledge for its own sake. Theology, like law and medicine, is what Schleiermacher called a "positive science," a study whose component parts are distinguished from the regular sciences with which they are methodologically aligned (e.g., history or philosophy) and held together only by their common usefulness in the performance of some positive practical task. In the case of Christian theology, this task is the maintenance and furtherance of the Christian community: "church leadership," broadly conceived. The fact that theology is not a pure science but a practical one instead does not license any relaxation of the standards of critical scholarship. It only permits the focusing of one's critical attention upon the particular complex of phenomena and issues which must be studied if the church is to be given proper guidance.

An historical understanding of the Christian community from its origins to the present is one of the subordinate aims of theology, i.e., one of the things it must achieve in order to serve the needs of church leadership. But there are two other requisites, in Schleiermacher's view, each giving rise to its own theological discipline, making three disciplines in all. First, it is necessary to attain a grasp of the distinctive essence of Christianity as such—that abiding nature which seeks expression ever anew in the actual, historical career of the church, in its doctrine and life.

---

[10] Friedrich Schleiermacher, *Brief Outline on the Study of Theology*, tr. Terrence N. Tice (Richmond: John Knox Press, 1966), 71, n. 1 (quoted from the first edition).
[11] Schleiermacher, *Brief Outline*, 26.

Historical study alone will not disclose that essence, only its various expressions. At the same time, it cannot be identified without a consideration of the historical reality of the church, since Christianity is an historical phenomenon with identifiable origins, and not a timeless idea which might be discovered through introspection or speculation. What is needed is a procedure whereby we might determine what *sort* of phenomenon Christianity is; then see how it compares with other things of that sort; and finally isolate its distinctive individual essence, that which strives for realization in all its historical forms.[12] The discipline concerned with this task Schleiermacher calls *philosophical theology*—partly, he says, because of its connection with that study of human reality ("ethics" in his terminology) which is one of the two main branches of human knowledge or "philosophy" broadly speaking (the other branch is "physics," the study of the natural world), and partly because its work consists largely in the definition of concepts, a task traditionally associated with philosophy.[13]

If philosophical theology yields an understanding of the genuine essence of Christianity, while historical theology depicts its actual situation, the comparison of the historical reality with the essence is bound to produce "feelings of pleasure and displeasure" in those concerned with the welfare of the church.[14] The task of the third theological discipline, *practical theology*, is to enable them to translate those feelings into appropriate action. Practical theology is a reflection upon the conduct of church leadership, which aims at the formulation of rules for the various aspects of that leadership. It presupposes an understanding of the goals of leadership (derived from the comparison of "what is" with "what should be"), and is concerned with the question of how those goals are to be achieved.[15] It is, therefore, a kind of technology *(Technik),* intended to guide deliberative action—action which can be neither mechanical nor arbitrary, but which must be thought out on the basis of principles in a given situation.[16] Although practical theology is itself closer to technical

---

[12] Schleiermacher, *Brief Outline*, 29–30 (§§32–35); the three-step sequence is developed and followed in the Introduction to Schleiermacher's own dogmatics, *The Christian Faith*.

[13] Schleiermacher, *Brief Outline*, 25 (§24).

[14] Schleiermacher, *Brief Outline*, 91 (§257).

[15] See Friedrich Schleiermacher, *Die praktische Theologie nach den Grundsätzen der evangelischen Kirche im Zusammenhange dargestellt,* ed. Jacob Frerichs *(Sämmtliche Werke,* I, 13; Berlin: G. Reimer, 1850), 19; *Brief Outline,* 92 (§260).

[16] Schleiermacher, *Die praktische Theologie,* 25; *Brief Outline,* 25 (§25), 93 (§265). Neither "technology" nor "technique" quite captures the sense of *Technik* in this context. "Technology" rightly distinguishes practical theology from practice itself, and calls to mind its reflective character; "technique," on the other hand, is better at conveying the sense that the practice under consideration is something of an art. Another term Schleiermacher often uses in place of *Technik* in this connection is *Kunstlehre:* the "doctrine" of an art or craft. He applies both terms to hermeneutics as well as to practical theology; see, e.g. *Brief Outline,* 56–57 (§§132–133).

knowledge than to pure science, it is an integral part of the "positive science" of theology. Indeed, without it, theology would not exist, since it is its orientation to the task of church leadership, i.e., to the ongoing responsibility of Christians for "the ever purer presentation of the essence of Christianity in each new moment," which constitutes theology as a science.[17]

The foregoing sketch of Schleiermacher's proposal, brief as it is, indicates something of its diagnostic power and visionary character. It was a constructive response to the new theological situation. Instead of deploring the ongoing transformation of the theological disciplines into relatively autonomous critical disciplines, Schleiermacher regarded it as a promising development and attempted to help it along, meanwhile locating the "theological" character and unity of these disciplines neither in their method nor in their subject matter *per se*, but in their orientation to a particular purpose. This purpose of equipping persons for the task of church leadership cannot, in Schleiermacher's judgment, be realized if theological study is nothing more than the mastery of techniques, or if some narrow criterion of pastoral utility is applied to it. He would most likely have agreed with Edward Farley's observation concerning such technically-preoccupied study: "The more the external tasks [of ministry] themselves are focused on as the one and only *telos* of theological education, the less the minister becomes qualified to carry them out."[18] Church leadership does involve technical knowledge, for Schleiermacher; but technical knowledge alone does not constitute the capacity for leadership. Leadership involves knowing *what* to do, as well as how to do it. And knowing what to do requires an understanding of the situation in which one is acting, and of the norms by which one's action is to be directed. In Schleiermacher's view, such an understanding is achieved through participation in the inquiries he called historical and philosophical theology: fully critical (or, as he would say, "scientific") inquiries intended to yield genuine knowledge of the actual situation of the church and of its ideal nature, respectively. Church leadership requires both "scientific knowledge" and "practical instruction," then, related appropriately in the service of an "interest in Christianity."[19]

Schleiermacher's proposal as a whole did not win widespread acceptance. Indeed, there was very little direct response to it of any kind for several years. But gradually some of its more important features began to be echoed in other encyclopedic schemes, and—more significantly—in the self-understandings and procedures of the individual disciplines.

---

[17] Schleiermacher, *Brief Outline*, 45 (§84).
[18] Farley, *Theologia*, 128.
[19] Schleiermacher, *Brief Outline*, 20–21 (§§5, 8).

Undoubtedly Schleiermacher's own scheme both influenced these developments and was prophetic of them; the precise mixture of influence to prophecy need not concern us here. Few of his specific proposals were absolutely without precedent, even though the scheme as a whole was a novel synthesis.

One of the elements of Schleiermacher's vision which did come to be widely shared, not only as a feature of later encyclopedic schemes but also as a working principle, is the conviction that it is their common orientation toward church leadership, and not anything distinctive about their methods or subject matter, which identifies and unites the theological disciplines. On its positive side, this so-called "teleological" view was not original with Schleiermacher. It was implicit, at least, in the earliest Protestant designs for theological studies, and it was expressly and forcefully advocated in the Pietist movement under whose influence Schleiermacher himself was raised. What was not so common before Schleiermacher was the negative component, i.e., the claim that this practical orientation was the *only* thing which distinguished theology from the cognate secular studies, so that there were no "sacred" or intrinsically theological disciplines.

This view guaranteed, in principle, the freedom of these disciplines to pursue the dynamics of their own development as scholarly traditions of critical inquiry—a freedom which has been of enormous significance for contemporary theology, where circumstances have permitted its exercise. But the teleological view has also meant that, generally speaking, internal controls over the scope of theological inquiry have been replaced with external controls. If the only thing which makes an inquiry "theological" is the use to which it is put, then those engaged in the inquiry may easily find themselves under considerable pressure—whether self-imposed or externally applied—to produce useful knowledge. In Schleiermacher's own scheme, in which the concept of theology as a "positive science" gave its individual components their theological identity, there was nevertheless a high degree of internal organization and coherence both within and among those components. In Schleiermacher's plan, theology as a whole is oriented to "church leadership," to be sure; but what church leadership involves is to be determined—in principle at least—by the theological inquiry itself, and not by any external, non-theological factors (e.g., the expectations of congregations, judicatories, or church officials). It is, as we have seen, through the interplay between historical theology and philosophical theology—through the comparison of "what is" with "what should be"—that the actual tasks of church leadership for the present are to be discerned. Given these tasks, practical theology is then to work out the practical principles by which the conduct of church leadership is to be guided. There is a clear relationship here among the normative, descriptive, and technical dimensions of theology, which gives the whole process its coherence and inner directedness.

But when various particulars of Schleiermacher's scheme are abandoned, or never shared in the first place—for instance, his own understanding of the nature and function of "philosophical theology," or the organic view of the Christian tradition which underlies his account of historical theology—that internal coherence and direction are easily lost. The principal disciplines tend then to become radically independent enterprises, oriented simply toward the production of "scientific" knowledge—as each discipline understands that adjective—concerning their respective subjects. As a consequence, it is the context in which those enterprises find themselves, rather than any internal principle, which then shapes them. If that context is the education of prospective pastors for nineteenth-century Germany (or twentieth-century America), then the organization of each discipline, the choice of material, tasks, and problems, and the general understanding of what is significant work, will be determined largely by the reigning conception of what pastors need to know—reigning, that is, in the minds of those who are empowered to design curricula, to establish faculty positions and to make appointments to them, to determine standards for academic and pastoral certification, etc., and thus to shape the study of theology. The agenda of practical theology is then set, for example, not by a theological assessment of the task of church leadership, but by the understanding of pastoral ministry which those holding such power wish to promote. (That understanding may, of course, be theologically derived in part; but it may also be decisively affected by political interests, social pressures, and other such factors.) The agenda of the other disciplines undergoes a corresponding modification in the direction of producing knowledge which will be pastorally useful. Such has been the upshot of the drastically simplified "teleological view" of theological study which succeeded Schleiermacher's own far more complex understanding of the way in which theology is ordered to church leadership.

In other respects as well, Schleiermacher's reception was mixed. For the most part, the traditional fourfold scheme was retained by Schleiermacher's successors.[20] Few of them followed him in subsuming either biblical theology or dogmatics under historical theology, and the notion of a separate discipline of philosophical theology such as Schleiermacher had envisioned was likewise ignored or rejected. On the surface, at least, the fourfold pattern remained intact.

---

[20] A brief overview of the post-Schleiermacherian developments is offered in Farley, *Theologia*, ch. 5. A more thorough account is available in J. F. Räbiger, *Encyclopaedia of Theology*, I, tr. John MacPherson (Edinburgh: T. & T. Clark, 1884), §§6, 20. The reception of Schleiermacher's *Brief Outline* itself is carefully treated by Alfred Eckert, *Einführung in die Prinzipien und Methoden der evangelischen Theologie* (Leipzig: G. Strübig, 1909), ch. 2.

Beneath that surface, however, the transformations to which Schleiermacher's own plan was both a response and a contribution were continuing. Biblical study, though kept formally distinct from historical theology or church history, was nevertheless now an historical study itself in its methods and aims. The fact that the Bible was still regarded as somehow uniquely normative was taken to justify the disciplinary distinction; but the task of discovering its normative import was understood to be an historical task. J. S. Semler (1725–1791) had proposed the decisive formulation a generation before Schleiermacher: given our historical understanding of the Bible, one should no longer say that the Bible *is* the Word of God, but rather, that it *contains* the Word of God.[21] It cannot be rightly interpreted by any direct, ahistorical exegesis which proposes to take it literally, i.e., as a text. It must instead be approached historically, as a collection of documentary sources out of which "the Word of God" (a phrase now clearly a metaphor for scripture's normatively significant content) is to be recovered or reconstructed. Of course, once one makes that move from "is" to "contains," discarding the orthodox theories of revelation and inspiration which guarded the uniqueness of scripture, the boundary between scripture and tradition fades, and with it—as Schleiermacher saw—the justification for anything but a relative distinction between "exegetical theology" and the study of the church's subsequent history. To the extent that this was recognized by his successors, their maintenance of separate biblical and historical divisions became more a matter of practical convenience than of principle.

Dogmatic theology, meanwhile, continued to be shaped as much by the concern to establish the credibility of Christian faith by relating it to what was perceived to be the real world as by the traditional task of expounding its doctrinal content. That is to say, it continued to combine the tasks which Schleiermacher had assigned separately to philosophical theology and to the historical discipline of dogmatics. Schleiermacher's own separation of the two was not intended to deny that a "philosophical" account of the nature of Christianity must be informed by history, nor that the constructive task of dogmatics requires some degree of philosophical reflection. But his scheme gave rise to misconceptions: It was widely believed that Schleiermacher had made theology "completely depen-

---

[21] On Semler's development of this principle, see Gottfried Hornig, *Die Anfänge der historisch-kritischen Theologie* (Göttingen: Vandenhoek und Ruprecht, 1961), ch. 4. This is really only a specification (and perhaps an unnecessarily restrictive one) of a more general principle, compatible with a wider variety of understandings of the nature and function of scripture, which Semler also derives from Luther: that the church's decision as to what is "canonical" must always be regarded as a provisional, human decision, subject to correction in light of later experience. Exegesis therefore cannot presuppose the legitimacy of any dogmatic decision as to the character or content of scripture; rather, dogmatic decisions must be based upon exegesis. This principle presents the more fundamental challenge to any *a priori* division between biblical and historical theology.

dent" upon philosophy (as one critic put it[22]), since it is philosophical theology which determines the essence of Christianity; and that his placing of both exegetical and dogmatic theology within historical theology amounted to a surrender of any stable norms for the faith. Truth and falsity are intermixed in these popular impressions. At any rate, it was generally thought that the old fourfold pattern could function as a safeguard against these Schleiermacherian tendencies, especially when it is arranged in such a way as to indicate the stages and the direction of theological thinking: Biblical study is given chronological and symbolic priority, as dealing with the normative beginnings of Christianity; history deals with its less normative, but still significant, subsequent development; systematic theology (a term which, in this period, usually embraces both dogmatics and ethics in its strictest use, but which is also commonly substituted for dogmatics alone) offers a rational account of the faith for the present moment; and practical theology, drawing its principles from systematic theology, offers guidance for churchly action.

Systematic theology, on this understanding, involves both historical and philosophical reflection: it is from Christian history (inclusive of the normative beginnings recorded in scripture) that it derives its data regarding the content of the Christian faith, and it is with the aid of some philosophical conceptuality that it interprets and arranges those data into an intelligible account of that faith—a system of Christian doctrine.[23] Systematic theology has the task of mediating between the historically "given" faith and the modern world. This understanding of the task was explicitly embraced by the so-called "mediating theologians" of the nineteenth century, and it continues to be the dominant understanding among major contemporary systematic theologians.[24]

---

[22] Räbiger, *Encyclopedia*, 91.

[23] There were, and are, stronger and weaker senses of "system" in this connection. The name of "systematic theology" has been applied to a considerable variety of enterprises since it originated, apparently in the sixteenth century. Otto Ritschl, *System und systematische Methode in der Geschichte des wissenschaftlichen Sprachgebrauchs und der philosophischen Methodologie* (Bonn: A. Marcus und E. Weber, 1903), provides a useful history of the principal transitions to his own day. In the earliest Protestant uses, a "system" of doctrine or theology was simply a coherent and reasonably detailed presentation of Christian teaching, organized so as to be useful to those preparing for pastoral office. "System" referred primarily to the method of presentation. Later, "system" came to be taken to refer to a quality of the material presented: Christian truth was thought to be "systematic," an organic unity, in itself, and the task of systematic theology was to exhibit that intrinsic character of the doctrinal *corpus*. Under the influence of Christian Wolff and others, a systematic account of something came to mean an account which subsumed everything in it under one principal idea: every system has a single "principle." With the decline of Wolffianism, the earlier, less stringent senses of "system" were again revived, though his was not entirely abandoned. All the variants remain in circulation, so that some care must be taken to understand just what is is that an advocate or opponent of "systematic theology" is advocating or opposing.

[24] An influential and widely-quoted formula is that of Schubert M. Ogden, "What Is Theology?", *The Journal of Religion*, 52 (1972), 22–40, in which theological statements are held to be subject to assessment by two criteria: "appropriateness" (faithfulness to what is normative in the tradition) and "understandability" (satisfaction of universally valid rele-

Practical theology, as the next step in the sequence, inherits the results of systematic theology, finding in (or fashioning from) those results its own principles of knowledge. In Schleiermacher's proposal, it will be recalled, practical theology was essentially a technology, not a science. Its task—as distinct from the other disciplines—was not to produce knowledge *(Kenntnisse)*, but to produce technical rules *(Kunstregeln)*.[25] Its status as an academic discipline was not, in Schleiermacher's view, dependent upon its possessing a "scientific" character in itself, but rather upon the fact that it was a necessary constituent part of the "positive science" of Christian theology.

But Schleiermacher's overall scheme for the organization of knowledge, including his concept of a positive science, was not widely adopted; and those who wished to preserve a place for practical theology in the academic curriculum generally thought it necessary to argue that it was more than *Technik*—that it was indeed a science, productive of genuine knowledge (of the church's present actuality, or of its tasks, or of its activity).[26] Whatever rules or principles of *action* practical theology might produce followed from principles of *knowledge* which were its prior products, and not simply its legacy from systematic theology. If one were to ask (as one practical theologian, Christian Palmer, eventually did[27]) in what way that knowledge or its production distinguished practical theology from systematic theology, the answers would be various and largely unsatisfying, because in most cases the "theoretical" component of practical theology was in fact indistinguishable from the corresponding elements of systematic theology, with its doctrines of the church, ministry, sacraments, etc.

Palmer himself suggested an answer which—perhaps because it was embedded in another unconventional encyclopedic scheme—did not receive the attention it deserved: that practical theology's knowledge is derived in part from practical experience, and from the study of actual practice, with attention to the conditions and context of that practice. Practical theology is not simply the application of knowledge derived from theoretical disciplines; it also involves the *attainment* of knowledge through concrete practical experience.[28] Although Palmer's voice was little heeded, other versions of this suggestion have greatly influenced both the conduct and the self-description of practical theology in recent decades, as the various practical specialties have drawn upon the resources of the social sciences to enhance their understandings of the areas in question. The relationship of this empirically-based knowledge,

[25] Schleiermacher, *Die praktische Theologie*, 17.

[26] Dietrich Rössler, "Prolegomena zur Praktischen Theologie: Das Vermächtnis Christian Palmers," *Zeitschrift für Theologie und Kirche*, 64 (1967), 359–362.

[27] Christian Palmer, "Zur praktischen Theologie," *Jahrbücher für Deutsche Theologie*, 1 (1856), 321.

[28] Palmer, "Zur praktischen Theologie," 337–345; cf. Rössler, "Prolegomena," 369–70.

with its attendant theories, to the accounts of the human condition, the church and its ministry, etc., which systematic theology formulates, has been a matter for continuing discussion. More recently still, the relationship between theological reflection and actual practice (or *praxis*) has come under renewed scrutiny from a number of directions. Practical theology is currently the focus of lively debate. The relationship of "theory" and "practice" within practical theology, the aptness of those terms themselves, and the relationship of practical theology to other disciplines and to churchly practice, are all under intense discussion.[29] The questions being raised are such that the discussion cannot be confined to the field of practical theology: the aims and procedures of the other theological disciplines are also in question, and it may be that the fourfold pattern with its ways of structuring the relation of knowledge and practice is facing its first really effective challenge.

There have been other challenges, to be sure. Karl Barth's threefold scheme of biblical, dogmatic, and practical theology was one such, coming as a part of his fundamental challenge to the whole liberal tradition of mediating theology. He called for a biblical theology which was not simply identical with critical historical exegesis, for a dogmatics which did not capitulate to a philosophical system, and for a practical theology which genuinely proceeded from biblical and dogmatic theology. In so doing, he identified some of the most vulnerable points of the inherited arrangement.[30] But, although his proposal was echoed by a few others, and influenced the self-understanding and procedures of some scholars in each of the major disciplines, it did not have great impact upon the fundamental structure and organization of theological study. Other proposals, earlier and later, have had still less influence. The post-Schleiermacherian modification of the fourfold pattern has remained reasonably secure.

As we have seen, that modification has produced what is in effect a threefold pattern: historical, "systematic," and practical. Biblical study belongs to the first, although it is normally separated out for convenience. The three divisions are methodologically distinct, the first being oriented to critical historical study, the second being principally philosophical, and the third taking its bearings from the so-called human sciences (sociology, psychology, etc.). Those alliances with the three secular disciplines or fields may account in part for the tenacity of this arrangement, since they have given each division a scholarly identity, rooting it in a tradition of inquiry. There may also be a deeper reason,

---

[29] For a sampling of current discussion, see the collection *Practical Theology: The Emerging Field in Theology, Church, and World*, ed. Don S. Browning (San Francisco: Harper & Row, 1983).

[30] See, e.g., Karl Barth, *Church Dogmatics*, I/1, tr. G. W. Bromiley (Edinburgh: T. & T. Clark, 1975), 4–5.

having to do with the nature of the subject-matter—the Christian tradition, Christian witness, the church—upon which theology reflects. This subject-matter may, in effect, demand a three-level or three-dimensional scrutiny, in which it is examined first with respect to its origin, then with respect to its content, and finally with respect to its goal. We shall return to this possibility in the chapters which follow. Whatever the reasons may be—and undoubtedly they are a heterogenous mixture—the fact is that the modified fourfold scheme still serves as the dominant structural and methodological context for the academic study of theology.

The purpose of this first chapter has been simply to set out this context—to trace its development, and in so doing to indicate something of its strengths and its problems. The account of the nature, structure, dynamics, and aims of Christian theology offered in the following chapters has been largely shaped by critical reflection upon that context. It may be seen as an attempt to appropriate its strengths and to address its problems, and thus to contribute in some manner to the formation of a new context for theological study.

Chapter II
Theology as Critical Inquiry

Christian theology may be defined as a critical inquiry into the validity of Christian witness.

"Christian witness" is meant here in a comprehensive sense, roughly equivalent to a similarly broad sense of "Christian tradition," that is, one embracing both the activity of bearing witness (or handing on the tradition) and the substance of what is borne or handed on. A further consideration of this concept will occupy us in the next chapter. The meaning of "validity"—likewise a comprehensive and complex notion here, and obviously a crucial one—will also come in for investigation then. Our present task is to consider what is involved in understanding theology as a critical inquiry.

An inquiry is an activity in which the answers to certain questions are sought. There are simple inquiries, in which the task is completed upon receiving a single answer to a single question. "What time is it?" "Three o'clock." And there are complex inquiries, in which the answer to the principal, leading question or questions can only be found by formulating and seeking answers to many other questions, and in which careful consideration must be given to the structure and procedure of the inquiry. In some inquiries, the question is simple, but seeking the answer is a lifelong activity; in others, framing the question is the most difficult part. Some inquiries can be resolved merely by reflecting upon what one already knows. Others require research, of one sort or another. Some demand a serious self-investment on the part of the inquirer, a willingness to submit to new experiences, perhaps even to become a different sort of person. Others make no such demand. There are inquiries with a definite conclusion, and inquiries which continue indefinitely, outlasting generations of inquirers. Some inquiries maintain a steady course, while others are in a constant process of revision as their questions and methods are themselves scrutinized.

The philosopher Wilfrid Sellars has written that "the aim of philosophy, abstractly formulated, is to understand how things in the broadest possible sense of the term hang together in the broadest possible sense of the term."[1] Philosophy, so described, is a very complex inquiry, in which

---

[1] Wilfrid Sellars, *Science, Perception and Reality* (London: Routledge & Kegan Paul, 1963), 1.

some very general questions about things and their possible relationships (and about such concepts as "thing" and "relationship") lead to
more specific questions about particular sorts of things and relationships, and in which these questions are themselves constantly examined and revised. It is an inquiry which makes definite demands upon
the serious inquirer. It is likely to remain an open inquiry: although
philosophers will sometimes offer accounts of how things hang together
(and will occasionally even claim to have given the definitive account),
such accounts, if taken seriously, immediately generate criticism and
further inquiry. Philosophers and philosophies come and go, but philosophy continues. It is perhaps the most comprehensive and open-
ended of all human inquiries.

Christian theological inquiry, as we shall see, has a philosophical dimension, and so partakes of the comprehensive and open-ended
character of philosophical inquiry in that respect. But Christian theology
is at the same time a broader and a more narrowly focused enterprise
than philosophy as such. It is more narrowly focused because its object,
Christian witness, is a delimited one, however vast, varied, and complicated; and it is broader because the question it raises concerning that
object, i.e., the question of its validity, has more than a philosophical
dimension.

Christian theology does not have exclusive rights to the name of
theology. There are, for example, theologies which bear somewhat the
same relationship to another religious tradition that Christian theology
bears to the Christian tradition (e.g., Jewish theology), and there are
theologies which are not essentially related to any particular tradition,
though they may make use of ideas derived from one or more traditions
(e.g., so-called "natural" or "philosophical" theologies). All these can
demonstrate some proper claim to the title of "theology," i.e., some way
in which they are centrally concerned with the question of right thought
and speech *(logos)* of God *(theos)*.[2]

There are also many other sorts of inquiries into the Christian tradition, or specific aspects of it, besides the theological sort: psychological,
economic, political, literary, and so on. These other inquiries do not
necessarily conflict or compete with theological inquiry, any more, say,
than a literary study of Plato's dialogues conflicts with their philosophical

---

[2] A critical inquiry into the validity of Christian witness is similarly entitled to the name
of "theology" only because the witness into which it inquires is a witness concerning God.
Christian witness itself is "theology" in the straightforward sense of "God-talk." When we
go on to distinguish theology from witness, it is not to deny the legitimacy of that
straightforward sense, but only to distinguish rational reflection upon witness from witness
itself. This ambiguity in the term "theology" goes back to its pre-Christian usage, and is
rooted in the fact that *logos* can mean either speech (discourse, etc.) or thought (reflection,
etc.).

evaluation. Indeed, just as an analysis of the literary character of a Platonic dialogue may aid a grasp of its philosophical argument, so these other approaches to Christian witness often contribute in one way or another to theological understanding. Even inquiries whose presuppositions or procedures appear inimical to Christian faith (e.g., a Marxist analysis of some episode in church history or of some contemporary church activity) may be theologically useful, perhaps by supplying new data or by raising important questions. Theology cannot simply adopt the procedures and results of these other inquiries, any more than it can simply dismiss them. In each case, the possible bearing of the inquiry upon the theological task needs careful assessment.

Christian theology is distinguished from other inquiries by its concern with the complex question of the validity of Christian witness. This concern identifies it as a *critical* inquiry, that is, one whose aim is to make certain sorts of judgments concerning its subject-matter. A critical inquiry generally has as its subject-matter some prior, ongoing human activity. It aims to bring that activity to reflective awareness, and in particular to identify and apply some appropriate standards of judgment (criteria) to the activity and its products. It is this concern with reflection, with the formation of reasoned judgments, which marks an inquiry as critical. It should not be thought that a critical inquiry is primarily negative in its intentions or effects, or even that its work consists only in making judgments, positive or negative, upon what has already been done or said. It can and often does include a constructive aspect—the making of imaginative judgments or proposals for the further conduct of the activity under scrutiny. John Passmore observes that since " 'critical thinking' may suggest nothing more than the capacity to think up objections," the actual course of critical thought might be better represented by a term such as "critico-creative" thinking: "Critical thinking as it is exhibited in the great traditions conjoins imagination and criticism in a single form of thinking: in literature, science, history, philosophy or technology the free flow of the imagination is controlled by criticism and criticisms are transformed into a new way of looking at things."[3] To call Christian theology a critical inquiry is certainly not to deny its creative character, or to play down the importance of that creativity. Theology has continually influenced the Christian tradition as the positive proposals issuing from theological reflection have been incorporated into every part of the church's life: creed, liturgy, law, pastoral practice, social action, institutional reform, and the rest. As critical reflection upon the church's activity, theology is as much concerned with its prospective activity as with its history. Indeed, it is for the

---

[3] John Passmore, "On Teaching to be Critical," in *The Concept of Education*, ed. R. S. Peters (London: Routledge & Kegan Paul, 1967), 201.

sake of the future that the church undertakes theological reflection upon its past.

Critical inquiry is sometimes called a "second-order" enterprise, to distinguish it from the "first-order" activity and discourse which is its given subject matter. Thus, as literary criticism stands to literature, so theology, as critical inquiry, stands to Christian witness. The application of this distinction to theology has both strengths and liabilities. It rightly indicates that Christian theology as such is not Christian witness, but rather a *study* of that witness—a study which may serve the cause of witness, but which can only do so when it is not confused with the activity of witness itself. This is a vital point, and one that is often obscured. Theology as such is not witness, not even of a refined and sophisticated sort. It is rather an attempt to bring witness to reflection, and to ask about its validity—its faithfulness, its truth, its aptness to its circumstances. The engagement of Christians in theological reflection might best be seen as an exercise in self-criticism, aimed at enabling those so engaged to bear more adequate witness. It involves the raising of some hard questions concerning one's own or one's church's present activities, understandings, and commitments. It may, of course, be decidedly inconvenient to disengage (if only in thought) from those activities, understandings, and commitments sufficiently to entertain serious critical reflection upon them. One might wish for a form of theology which was more directly and uncritically affirmative of one's present leanings, furnishing a rationale for decisions already made rather than insisting on bringing those decisions under scrutiny. Certainly such rationalization has gone on under the name of theology often enough. In such instances, theology has been more nearly an extension of witness than an examination of it. To recognize theology as a "second-order" endeavor is to guard against that misuse. It is to acknowledge that theology can make its distinctive and vital contribution to Christian witness only when it is distinguished in principle from it. Theology is a reflective moment within the Christian life, when that life is examined and when judgments are reached bearing on its past and future. As such, theology is an aspect of the continuing repentance to which the church and all its members are called.

As this latter point suggests, the "first-order"–"second-order" distinction should not be applied in such a way as to force a separation between theology and witness. They are clearly interdependent, and the distinction between them is strictly a functional one. It should not be construed as a distinction between the "scholarly" and the "popular," for although there is and should be scholarly theological inquiry, there is also a theological element, a process of reflection and judgment, within Christian life as such. It should not be taken as a distinction between two forms of discourse, as if one could tell by looking at a statement whether it belongs to "theology" or "witness." Countless statements can serve, and indeed have served, both functions, having a place within theological discourse on one occasion, and being used to convey the Christian message on another. It is, to repeat, a functional distinction, and function may not always be discerned from form. One must look to the situation, and to what is being done. When Christian witness is being examined as to its validity, there is theology. When Christian witness is actually being advocated or performed, there is witness.

Of course, the two activities are generally somehow concurrent. One does not—or at any rate, should not—terminate theological reflection when witness begins. Rather, reflection accompanies practice, continuing to guide it as circumstances call for fresh judgments. (This does not mean that one is to be "reflective" at every moment. That could be as inhibiting to good practice in this case as it would be in the case of a dancer or a surgeon. Part of one's competence lies in knowing when reflection is called for, and in being able to combine reflection with appropriate attention to the immediate situation.) Likewise, theological reflection itself is often enhanced by participation in witness. Just as there are advantages to be realized sometimes by getting some distance from the object of one's reflection, so as to lessen the distortions in perception and judgment which may accompany personal involvement or a too-narrow focus, so there are advantages to be realized precisely *through* personal involvement. One can often gain a clearer sense of the situation, can see the point of a given act or utterance, or can have one's perceptual and conceptual abilities sharpened through actual engagement in the practice which one is trying to understand. We ought not to choose between distance and participation, deciding that only one of them is the proper stance for theological inquiry. Both are needed. But theology's need for engagement as well as distance, just as witness's need for reflection as well as advocacy, should not obscure the distinction between theology and witness. To the extent that the "first-order"–"second-order" terminology contributes to the maintenance of any of the false contrasts just mentioned, its use must be guarded.

To call theology a critical inquiry does not yet distinguish it sufficiently from other critical inquiries into the same subject-matter. It does not yet indicate what sort of criticism is involved, nor to what end. Criticism comes in many varieties. A philosopher's account of how things hang together, for instance, might be criticized in several ways, depending on one's interests: Is it well written? Does it really represent the way things hang together? Is it the best such account given the philosopher's principles? Does it give proper support to the class struggle (or to free enterprise)? Is it consistent with the church's teaching? Some of these questions might represent or help to constitute *philosophical* criticism, i.e., an effort to judge the account as a philosophical account. (Whether these questions have been aptly formulated to achieve this end is another question—likewise a philosophical one.) Others obviously represent other modes of criticism, e.g., literary or political criticism. These other modes of criticism, though non-philosophical, are not necessarily illegitimate. One may evaluate a philosophical work *as* philosophy, but one may also evaluate it *as* literature, *as* a political statement, and so on. These modes of criticism should not be isolated from each other, since they can be mutually illuminating; but they should not be confused with each other. The important thing in any case is to be clear as to the relationship between one's aims and one's procedures.

Christian witness can likewise be critically appraised in any number of ways. The sermons of Jonathan Edwards may be read as literature; the reliability of the synoptic gospels as historical sources may be assessed; the rhetorical style or the production techniques of a television evangelist may be studied; the political impact of the Roman Catholic church upon contemporary Poland may be evaluated. Christian witness may be criticized *as* literature, *as* history, and so forth. It can also be criticized *as* Christian witness; and it is *this* criticism that is the distinctive task of Christian theology. That is, Christian theology seeks to judge any given sample of Christian witness—past, present, or prospective—by the standards which pertain to it precisely as Christian witness. In the definition of Christian theology given at the outset, this is what was meant by calling it a critical inquiry into the *validity* of Christian witness.

As noted, this is a complex assignment. It may involve, in a given instance, inquiring into such diverse things as historical accuracy, production techniques, and political impact. Answering the question of the validity of witness requires posing and answering a variety of subordinate questions which stand in complex relationships to each other. The next chapter will attempt to identify and relate three dimensions of theological inquiry, three main lines of questioning, each with its own proper structure and procedures. These three, taken together and related appropriately, comprise that inquiry into the validity of Christian witness which is Christian theology.

But first it would be well to deal at least in a provisional way with the question of the relationship of an understanding of theology as critical inquiry to some other prominent uses of the term "theology." That there is such a thing as theological inquiry may seem beyond dispute. (It has not always seemed so, especially if "inquiry" is taken to mean "*critical* inquiry," though of course there have long been theological questions and answers. At times, "critical theological inquiry" would have seemed a contradiction in terms—as it may still, for some.) But that one ought to think of theology *primarily* as such an inquiry—that this is the first or proper sense of "theology"—has not been so obvious. In fact, other senses of the term have usually prevailed.

There have been times in both Protestant and Roman Catholic history when theology was thought of primarily as a *habitus*, a habit (in the technical sense of "habit," meaning something like "aptitude" or "disposition," derived primarily from Aristotle and much employed in traditional discussions of human nature), and when much attention was given to specifying the sort of habit theology is. For the early and exemplary Lutheran writer Johann Gerhard, for example, theology was a practical intellectual *habitus*, like wisdom *(sapientia)*—except that theology is, in a special sense, a God-given capacity and distinct from all ordinary human wisdom. "Wisdom" is still the nearest available category in Gerhard's psychology. Using a different vocabulary from that of *habitus*, one might make Gerhard's point by calling theology an "understanding": a set of conceptual capacities with which a person tends to engage reality or a certain aspect of it, in this case, one's relationship to God and all that that involves. Theology as *habitus* belongs to faith, as its intellectual or cognitive component—not its "objective" intellectual component, i.e., beliefs, but rather the believing of them, when that gets beyond the mere holding of opinions (which in Gerhard's time was called *fides historica*) and becomes a matter of self-forming conviction or existential "self-understanding." In Gerhard's view, pastors and teachers require more of this aptitude, a fuller and more accurate understanding, than ordinary believers, so as to give proper guidance to those in their charge; but though there is a difference in degree, there is no difference in kind between this more rigorous theology and simple believing.[4]

Regarding the *habitus* of theology as God-given did not prevent Gerhard and others from acknowledging that its acquisition involves effort, but it did encourage an emphasis on some traditional means of theological understanding—e.g., the path of *oratio, meditatio,* and *tentatio* (prayer, meditation, and "testing") which Luther had commended. These could themselves be regarded as especially God-given means of understanding, distinct from ordinary human efforts. At the same time, they seemed especially suited by their nature to the development of the intellectual disposition appropriate to faith. A practice guided by these principles becomes a venture of self-transformation in obedience to the Word of God in scripture. The emphasis is on the inquirer's self-involvement with the text or doctrine under study: on receptivity to its truth, and on a willingness to be guided and affected by it in mind and heart so that one's understanding is formed by it. It is not simply the text that is

---

[4]See Johannes Wallmann, *Der Theologiebegriff bei Johann Gerhard und Georg Calixt* (Tübingen: J. C. B. Mohr [Paul Siebeck], 1961), 71–75.

understood in such a practice: it is the self and the world that are understood, with the text serving, by God's grace, as the instrument of understanding. The importance of certain sorts of factual or technical knowledge (e.g., of languages, geography, human behavior, and so forth) for the correct interpretation of scripture and tradition was rarely denied, but it was clear that such knowledge, objective in character and gained by ordinary means, was not constitutive of real theological understanding.[5] Too much interest in such technical pursuits was often regarded as dangerous, not only because it concentrated on the wrong things but because it was the wrong sort of concentration: secular rather than sacred, "objectifying" rather than self-involving, an attempt to grasp and use the facts at one's disposal about a text of scripture or a doctrinal statement through the scholarly methods which are suited to deal with such facts, rather than to put oneself at God's disposal through prayerful meditation upon what is given there.

The potential for conflict between the two approaches to scripture or doctrine just mentioned has long been felt. In the twelfth century, it was manifested in the conflict between the older tradition of *lectio divina*, the gradual absorption of the meaning of scripture through slow, patient, meditative reading, as practiced in the monasteries, and the newer approach to scripture and doctrine through the methods practiced in the liberal arts in the schools which were to become the first universities.[6] It was the difference between "discipline" in the monastic or devotional sense and "discipline" in the scholarly sense: what, it was frequently asked, does the latter have to do with theology, that is, with the intellectual disposition of faith? In much Protestant dogmatics since the seventeenth century, the same tension has been evident in the way "theology" and "philosophy" have been related (and often opposed) to each other. Here, as among the defenders of *lectio divina* in the earlier period, the impression is sometimes given that one may be receptive to scripture and obedient to God, or one may ask irrelevant questions. The former path leads to the cultivation of the theological *habitus,* that is, to a proper understanding of divine things, while the latter leads only to perdition.

The notion of theology as a critical inquiry seems distant indeed from this view of theology—not only different, but hostile, insofar as the formation of the theological *habitus* has been understood to involve some of the very practices and attitudes of which the modern critical spirit has been most suspicious: submission of the intellect to authority, emotional involvement, credulousness, etc. There is a genuine conflict here, and one whose resolution, if it comes, will involve sorting out what is really at

---

[5] *Ibid.,* 33–45.

[6] See G. R. Evans, *Old Arts and New Theology: The Beginnings of Theology as an Academic Discipline* (Oxford: Clarendon Press, 1980), chapter 1, esp. 44–45.

stake in both approaches. For instance, one undeniable truth in the older position is that theological understanding involves not only the manipulation and mastery of objective data, but also the extension and enrichment or even transformation of one's own subjectivity. It calls for a kind of conceptual growth which is not narrowly intellectual, but which, by the nature of the concepts involved, touches on other dimensions of selfhood. Whether theology can properly be characterized as critical inquiry depends in part on whether the concept of critical inquiry can be broad enough to encompass, rather than ignore or oppose, this aspect of theological understanding, and thus do justice to a central insight of the older tradition.

There is, to be sure, a common view of what critical thinking involves which would rule out this possibility. Here the tension between the sort of engagement necessary to acquire an understanding of the Christian faith and the sort of distancing necessary to reflection upon the nature and adequacy of that understanding is made into an opposition: faithful obedience versus prideful autonomy (if you favor the first), or immature dependence versus responsible reflection (if you favor the second). Those who favor either pole do not need to look far to find instances of the corresponding abuse. Some of the ways in which the older tradition guarded its insight into the understanding of faith and fostered the appropriate practice also fostered an uncritical traditionalism, and discouraged the raising of important questions as to the validity of what was being represented as the substance of the Christian witness. And when critical questions about the meaning and truth of that witness, the history and credibility of scripture, the claims of the church to continuity with its origins and to divine sanction, and so forth were eventually raised from outside and pressed upon the church, it was in part that older tradition of theology which left the church dismally unprepared to deal with them. At the same time, there can be no doubt that a theology imbued with the modern critical spirit has sometimes been quick to judge what it has not yet understood. In such instances, the problem is probably not that the theology was "too critical," but rather that it was not critical enough: insufficiently critical of its own understanding, perhaps, or insufficiently reflective concerning its own methodology. At any rate, an adequate understanding of theology as critical inquiry must be one which overcomes the apparent opposition between engagement and reflection, and incorporates both in a fully critical approach.

The tradition of regarding the theological *habitus* as the primary or proper sense of "theology" survives in some conservative theological circles—often accompanied by the usual suspicion of critical inquiry. But a more widespread current alternative both to the *habitus* sense and to the notion of theology as inquiry is to treat what is sometimes called the objective, rather than the subjective, sense of the term "theology" as its primary sense; that is, to use the term to designate that which is known or believed, rather than either the knowing or believing of it (the *habitus*) or the process of its acquisition and testing. Ordinarily, when someone refers to the theology of a particular person or group, what is meant is neither the theological aptitude nor the theological activity of that person or group, but rather the ideas or positions held. "Theology" here is a synonym for "doctrine" or "teachings" or "beliefs" or "opinion"—for the outcome of theological reflection, perhaps, but not for the reflection itself, nor for whatever *habitus* it may involve or inform. Broadly speaking, this objective sense of theology may embrace every articulation of faith in the Christian tradition from the apostles onwards, from official church teachings (confessions, creeds, etc.) to unofficial statements, from the spontaneous witness of the so-called simple believer to the most carefully refined critical judgments of the professional theologian. Used more narrowly, it typically refers to the product of some deliberate and methodically stringent effort at theological reflection, and is distinguished as such from the ordinary, less reflective exercise of Christian witness.

Even though, in this narrower usage, theology in the objective sense is regarded as the product of theological reflection, the focus is still kept on the product rather than on the reflective process. A student who thinks of theology in this way is thus likely to regard a theological textbook as a body of knowledge, or at least of opinion; it is no doubt recognized as the fruit of someone's reflection, but it is seen less as a guide to the process of reflection than as a presentation of "ideas." Its principal aim, it is supposed, is to convey information. (This supposition may be contrary to the intentions of the author of the textbook, and of the instructor who uses it; but of course it may also be reinforced, subtly and even unwittingly, by both.) If in the older tradition the study of theology was essentially a matter of acquiring the theological *habitus*, in this alternative view it tends to be seen as the enterprise of acquiring objective knowledge, and perhaps thereby acquiring a more sophisticated set of beliefs about God, creation, etc.

When this sense of the term "theology" prevails, along with a corresponding view of theological study, a question naturally arises as to its point—particularly in a course of study primarily intended to prepare persons to exercise responsible leadership in the church. That is, while this sense of "theology" is apparently more readily reconcilable with the process of critical inquiry, its greatest difficulty comes just at the point where the traditional approach seemed to have its greatest strength. Theology as *habitus*, and theological study as its development, have some obvious pertinence to Christian life and ministry. But the value of a knowledge of the views of various theologians is not always apparent, even if one comes to share some of those views. Occasionally a student or graduate comes to learn this the hard way, by trying to give a congregation the same sort of education. Most students are wise enough to realize that this is not their mission, but they too are left wondering what all this knowledge is for. In some cases, a theological education appears to serve only to alienate its recipients intellectually and affectively from the sort of community in which they were nurtured and in which they intend to work. Rather than equipping them for ministry, their knowledge has an incapacitating effect.

Where this sense of "theology" prevails, the question of the relevance of theology is likely to be pressing; and the common division (whether formally acknowledged or not) of the theological curriculum into a largely irrelevant if not downright dangerous component concerned with the acquisition of theological knowledge (the "academic" or "theoretical" part) and a more useful, if still unevenly effective component concerned with more practical preparation for life and leadership in the church (groups for spiritual formation, courses in pastoral functions, etc.) testifies that no very positive answer has so far emerged. Given the terms of the question, none is likely to emerge, and the irrelevance of theological theory to churchly practice becomes a byword.

This situation has led one recent writer to advocate a return to the older usage, in which the theological *habitus* was theology proper, and to urge the reorientation of theological study around this sense of the term. In his *Theologia: The Fragmentation and Unity of Theological Study,* and in other writings,[7] Edward Farley has argued that the cultivation of *theologia* (a term he associates primarily with theology as *habitus*) ought to be the primary aim of theological study. According to Farley, the ascendancy of an understanding of theology as objective knowledge, and the domination of theological education by scholarly disciplines geared to the production and dissemination of such knowledge, has led to the loss of *theologia,* to the consequent alienation of theory from practice, and to the general incoherence and inadequacy of contemporary theological education. In order to re-institute *theologia* and reform theological education around it, we must, in Farley's view, first come to an understanding of what "ecclesiality"—the mode of existence proper to the Christian community—involves; then determine what sort of *habitus* is requisite for the proper maintenance of ecclesiality, and for church leadership specifically; and then undertake the work of building a curriculum, perhaps

---

[7] Edward Farley, *Theologia: The Fragmentation and Unity of Theological Education* (Philadelphia: Fortress Press, 1983); "The Reform of Theological Education as a Theological Task," *Theological Education,* 17 (1981), 93–117; "Theology and Practice Outside the Clerical Paradigm," in *Practical Theology: The Emerging Field in Theology, Church, and World,* ed. Don S. Browning (San Francisco: Harper & Row, 1983), 21–41.

little resembling anything we have now, which would aim at the formation of that *habitus,* i.e., which would center in the teaching and learning
of *theologia.*

In Farley's usage, the term *theologia* may refer to the science or study in
which the theological *habitus* is formed and exercised, as well as to the
habitus itself. But he insists that *theologia* as science or study derives its
meaning and unity only from its association with the *habitus.* According
to Farley, "theology in its original and most authentic sense" refers to "a
sapiential and personal knowledge."[8] The individual theological disciplines as well as the enterprise of theological education are to be oriented
to the acquisition and transmission of this sapiential knowledge or
wisdom. When they focus instead upon objective knowledge, theology is
"dispersed," losing its authentic character as theology.

In his orientation of theology to the practical task of the formation of a
habitus, Farley's position bears some acknowledged resemblance to
Friedrich Schleiermacher's claim that the various disciplines which comprise theology find their theological identity and their unity only in their
common reference to the tasks of church leadership.[9] The chief difference, as Farley sees it, is that while Schleiermacher's solution leads to a
view of theology as culminating in a sort of technical knowledge but
leaves the constituent disciplines in their modern form basically untouched, his own solution presents *theologia* as a unified, practical
wisdom, intimately related to faith and to ecclesiality, and requires a
fundamental rethinking of the ways in which the individual disciplines
may contribute to its development.[10]

On Farley's view, then, a proper understanding of what theology is
may be found by moving from a phenomenological description of "ecclesiality" to a depiction of the *habitus* proper to it, and thence to an
account of the sorts of intellectual activity needed for the cultivation of
that *habitus,* either on the part of ordinary church members (thus *theologia* as the basis for church education) or on the part of church leaders
(thus *theologia* as the key to the renewal of professional theological
education).

Farley is surely correct in pointing out that the common emphasis on
the objective sense of the term "theology" is misplaced, and that this
misplaced emphasis is reinforced (however unwittingly) in much contemporary theological education. The development of genuine theological competence, with all that this involves by way of self-knowledge, the
extension of one's capacities as a human being, etc., as well as by way of

---

[8] Farley, *Theologia,* xi.

[9] Friedrich Schleiermacher, *Brief Outline on the Study of Theology,* tr. Terrence N. Tice
(Richmond, Virginia: John Knox Press, 1966), 20–21.

[10] See, e.g., *Theologia,* 127–128.

gaining a mastery of the methods of inquiry, is easily neglected in favor of a preoccupation with factual knowledge. Theological education is by no means unique in this regard; in nearly every field of study, education can quickly degenerate into the transmission of "facts" if there is not serious and constant attention to the much more difficult task of developing students' abilities. In theological education, as in other fields, the rapid expansion of pertinent knowledge simply increases the pressure on the curriculum to incorporate more data. It is essential to remember that knowledge of the Bible, of church history, of doctrinal schemes, of educational theory, of the church's social situation, and so forth, however useful or even necessary to a theological education, is not its ultimate aim. That aim, as Farley argues, is the development of a *habitus;* a particular competence, along with the disposition to exercise it.

To say that the proper aim of theological education is the development of a *habitus* (or, in less archaic language, of a particular competence and disposition) is not, however, to say that theology itself is best described as a *habitus.* If we were forced to choose between the so-called subjective and objective senses of "theology" and to designate one or the other as its primary sense, we might well side with Farley, and attempt to understand theology as well as theological education in terms of theological aptitude. But even to state that option is to reveal its chief difficulty, a difficulty which Farley goes on to illustrate in the course of his defense of it: to attempt to describe theology in terms of a theological *habitus* is to put the cart before the horse, for a *habitus* must itself be described in terms of that for which it is a *habitus.* One can, of course, say that to love is to exercise a loving disposition. But the inadequacy of this as a definition of "love" is immediately apparent, since a loving disposition can itself only be defined in terms of the acts, emotions, etc., which its possessor is disposed to do or to have. Just so, a theological aptitude can only be defined in terms of the activity for which it is an aptitude.

Farley himself recognizes this, in that he occasionally refers to the activities associated with the furtherance of "ecclesiality" as a way of indicating what sort of wisdom or understanding *theologia* is: it consists in an ability to interpret the Christian tradition, to acertain its truth, and to incorporate it into the contemporary situation.[11] He goes on to give a brief description of the dialectical movement of thought involving these three activities; and at this point he uncharacteristically refers to theological understanding itself as "an activity, a life process." Evidently what he has in mind here is what he has earlier described as the secondary sense of the premodern notion of *theologia*, which was lost along with the first:

---

[11] Farley, *Theologia*, 164. The three sorts of theological activity Farley describes here bear some resemblance to the three dimensions of theological inquiry to be depicted in our next chapter.

theologia as "a discipline of inquiry and study"—the activity corresponding to the *habitus*.[12] His intention appears to be to offer a sketch of the postmodern counterpart to this unitary theological science.

Although he finds himself thus referring to the activity of theology in order to describe the theological *habitus*, Farley does not recognize a major implication of this necessity: namely, that it is the activity of theology—theology as inquiry—which is theology in the primary sense. It is the "active" sense of the term which is prior; the "subjective" and "objective" senses are both derivative from it, both logically and chronologically. The theological *habitus* not only must be defined in terms of theological activity, it also can only be acquired through participation in that activity—a point which was never denied even by those like Gerhard who insisted most strongly on its God-given character.[13] Likewise, theology in its objective sense, as that which is known or believed, can only be understood as the product of theological activity, of some process of inquiry and judgment, whether of an elementary or a more advanced sort. To treat the so-called subjective and objective senses as exhaustive alternatives is to trap oneself in a dilemma.

Farley is entirely correct in claiming that the proper aim of theological education is the cultivation of the theological *habitus*—rightly understood. However, both the nature of that *habitus* and the character of the education required for its formation can be understood only by giving fuller attention to the character of theological inquiry. If the theological *habitus* really is the capacity and disposition to engage in theological inquiry, and if it is this that theological education is really meant to foster, then it seems reasonable to assume that some clarity concerning what theological inquiry involves is a requisite for understanding either one.

Those are both serious "ifs." The long-standing tension between a *habitus*-oriented theological tradition and the enterprise of critical theological inquiry has already been noted, along with the need for a reconsideration of both if they are to be effectively related. There are a number of issues here which must be sorted out. At the same time, it is by no means universally granted that "theological education" really means *theological* education—that it centers in the teaching and learning of theology. It can be and often is regarded simply as the collective term for the assortment of disparate things which make up a curriculum in what is conventionally called a theological school; or it can be taken as a synonym for "education for ministry"—and again the adjective "theolog-

---

[12] Farley, "Theology and Practice," 23–24; *Theologia*, 31–32.

[13] There may have been writers in this broad tradition who claimed that "the *habitus* originates partly from a supernatural gift and partly as an effort of inquiry," as Farley summarizes the relation (*Theologia*, 44); but one can imagine Gerhard, at least, having some difficulty with the division of labor suggested by that statement.

ical" implies nothing about the nature of the educational process, except perhaps that something called "theology" was once a prominent part of it.

Whether a clearer grasp of what theological inquiry involves really is the key to a proper understanding of theological education can only be discovered in the attempt. Accordingly, the task of the next two chapters is to offer an account of the structure and dynamics of theological inquiry. The succeeding chapter will then take up the question of the nature and aims of theological education in the light of this account.

Chapter III
Three Dimensions of Theology

An inquiry is constituted not by its subject matter alone, nor simply by the particular questions it puts to that subject matter, but by the aims which lead it to pursue certain questions with regard to certain material. The comprehensive aim of Christian theological inquiry is to test Christian witness by the criteria which pertain to its validity precisely as Christian witness. This aim is behind all the particular questions which theology asks concerning Christian witness, many of which are identical with questions which might be put in the course of other inquiries. It is the aim these questions serve which makes them (in a broad sense, at least) theological questions; and to identify them as theological is not to say that some of them might not also rightly be regarded as, say, philosophical or historical questions. The fact is that theology is an inquiry which includes other sorts of inquiry. It does not just involve individual questions which also happen to have a home in other inquiries; it incorporates these inquiries themselves. That is, one pursues a certain part of the theological task *by* engaging in historical inquiry, and another part *by* philosophical inquiry, and so on.

Theology is not simply a composite of these other inquiries, however. Rather, in each of its dimensions and in its totality, theological inquiry incorporates these others—without violating their own identity and integrity—into a larger whole which transcends their own particular aims. We must now see how this is.

There are three main sorts of questions involved in Christian theological inquiry. We might say that there are three principal questions which this inquiry raises concerning its subject matter, each of which is the leading question of a particular dimension of theology. Since the aim of theology is to examine the validity of Christian witness *as* Christian witness, i.e., according to its own intrinsic criteria, each of these leading questions may be seen to derive from a particular formal, constitutive feature of that witness. Together, they constitute a comprehensive inquiry into the validity of Christian witness as such. To develop this understanding of the plurality and unity of theology, it is necessary to turn to that further elucidation of the concept of Christian witness which was promised in the preceding chapter, and to show how the dimensions of theological inquiry correspond to its features.

It was noted then that the term "Christian witness" was intended in a broad sense, roughly equivalent to a similarly broad sense of the term "Christian tradition." Just as we may distinguish an "active" sense of the latter term, denoting the activity of transmitting, from a "passive" or "objective" sense, i.e., the substance or content which is transmitted, so we may distinguish two senses of "witness": the activity of bearing witness, and the witness which is being borne. (The corresponding Greek noun *marturia* likewise exhibits these two senses. *Martus*, also frequently translated "witness," refers to one who bears witness, while *marturia* designates either the activity or the content. It is with *marturia* that we are principally concerned here.[1])

In addition to its inclusion of both the active and the objective senses, the concept of Christian witness adopted here has breadth in two other ways. First, although "Christian witness" (or "the Christian witness") can be used as a normative concept—just as the adjective "Christian" can be used normatively, to mean something like "authentically Christian"—that is not its use here. Rather, it is intended to include anything and everything which represents itself as, or might plausibly be taken as intending to be, Christian witness. (Here, too, this use parallels a very broad sense of "Christian tradition.") Secondly, this witness may be nonverbal as well as verbal in character. In its most comprehensive sense, it embraces not only Christian doctrine and its dissemination, but everything the church is and does as the church—everything Christians are and do, insofar as it exhibits or signifies or even implies that which they have received from "Jesus Christ the faithful witness" (Rev. 1:5), and which is constitutive of their own being and mission as Christians. Hospitals and schools, political demonstrations and legislative lobbies, the pattern of one's personal life, and a great variety of other institutions, activities, and ways of being besides what we normally think of as "the church," may embody Christian witness in one way or another. It is with all of this that theology is properly concerned.

Because of some shared characteristics, "witness," "tradition," "church," and a few other terms can be used in roughly parallel ways in stating the theological task. Trading on the ambiguity created by the fact that each possesses a normative as well as an empirical sense, one may state the central question of theology in such ways as these: To what extent is Christian witness Christian witness? When is the church the church? Where is the tradition in the tradition? Christian theology is the self-criticism of the Christian community with regard to its own being and activity as Christian community. Although it has several functional parallels, "Christian witness" may be the most flexible and inclusive

[1] For a comprehensive study of the background and use of these and related terms in early Christianity, see H. Strathmann's account in the *Theological Dictionary of the New Testament*, vol. IV, ed. Gerhard Kittel, tr. Geoffrey W. Bromiley (Grand Rapids, MI: William B. Eerdmans Co., 1967), s.v. *martus, ktl.*.

single term for that being and activity. Furthermore, it lends itself readily to an analysis in which the various dimensions of the theological task may be explored.

As to the first of these dimensions: One of the illuminating formal features of the concept of Christian witness is that such witness is witness to Jesus Christ. It is not simply a matter of stating one's own convictions, but also one of representing the authentic Christian message in doing so. It necessarily involves an explicit or implicit claim (however qualified in recognition of human limitations, etc.) to represent this truly. But, of course, the attempt may be more or less successful, the claim more or less justified. The extent to which what is offered as Christian witness really is *Christian* witness, i.e., really does represent what it is intended to represent, cannot be measured by the good intentions of those bearing the witness, nor by their popularity, nor by any of a number of other standards which might readily suggest themselves. It pertains to theological inquiry to pursue the critical question which corresponds to this feature of Christian witness, with regard to any particular instance of it: Is it truly Christian? Is it genuinely entitled to that adjective? The question of the "Christianness" of any allegedly Christian witness is the first of our three principal theological questions.

The second principal question is provoked by the fact that, although Christian engaged in witness are not *simply* stating their convictions, they are stating their convictions. To bear witness is to represent something as the truth: to assert it, to commend it, to endorse it as worthy of acceptance. Whether or not this is at all explicit in a given instance, it is at least implicit in every genuine act of Christian witness (as distinguished from, say, a descriptive account of what Christians believe). It belongs to the concept of Christian witness that such a claim to truth is present. The critical theological question which corresponds to this feature of its object is, naturally enough: Is this witness really true? What claims to truth does it make or imply, and how are those claims to be judged? This is the central question of a second dimension of theological inquiry.

The third principal question corresponds to a third feature of the concept, already suggested by such terms as "commending" and "endorsing." Witness is not merely "expression" for its own sake, but rather an attempt to convey a message. The validity of an instance of Christian witness cannot be judged solely in terms of the intrinsic "Christianness" and truth of its content; because it is directed outwardly as an act of communication, its fitness to the context in which it is enacted must also be examined. Neither its Christian authenticity nor its truth, nor both together, are sufficient to render it valid as witness. Indeed, it is questionable whether an act of witness could even be assessed on either of these points at all apart from a consideration of its relationship to its context, since the meaning of an utterance or an act cannot be fully determined without taking its context into account. A speaker who is oblivious to context may be profoundly, though unintentionally, misleading. An act which conveys one message in one setting may be taken quite differently in another. There is a kind of fidelity to "tradition," an adherence to old forms and to the memory of old situations, which amounts to betrayal, just as there is a kind of freedom from and with tradition which permits a more genuine and radical faithfulness to it. Sometimes you can't say the same thing by saying the same thing; in order to say the same thing, you must say something different.

The critical question theology has to raise in response to this feature of Christian witness is: Is this witness fittingly enacted? Is it appropriately related to its context? Of course, what it means for an act of witness to be appropriately related to its context cannot be determined by a study of the context alone. The content and intention of Christian witness itself have some decisive bearing both on how the context is to be understood and on how it is to be aptly addressed. This means that the pursuit of this third principal theological question involves some grappling with the previous two, just as they themselves cannot be answered without some reference to this third dimension of the inquiry. The proper interplay among all three questions is vital to any attempt to deal with each of them.

Each of these three principal questions has been stated initially in a form appropriate to the designation of theology as a critical, "second-order" reflection upon some given sample or samples of witness. These are the questions theology addresses to, let us say, a sermon by Martin Luther, or the doctrinal decisions of some ecclesiastical body, or the social-action program of a local congregation. But each question may also be given constructive formulation. This is fortunate, since the need for a constructive formulation is encountered early on in the attempt to answer each of the critical questions in any case. Critical and constructive reflection are not opposed, but complementary moments of one process of thought, as Passmore's term, "critico-creative thinking," suggests. To the critical question, "Is this witness truly Christian?", there corresponds the constructive question, "What is truly Christian witness?" To the question, "Is this witness true?", there corresponds the question, "What is the truth of Christian witness?" And to "Is this witness fittingly enacted?" there corresponds "How is Christian witness fittingly enacted?"

The intention behind these constructive formulations is more modest than the questions themselves may suggest. They should not convey the impression that the goal of theological inquiry is some single, definitive, universally valid statement of the Christian witness. Their common point is simply this: judgment presupposes criteria. Whether one is attempting to judge the adequacy of some former instance of witness, or deliberating on a course of action for the future, one needs standards by which to judge. The search for what is constitutive of valid Christian witness is thus ingredient in the critico-creative inquiry, in each of its three basic dimensions.

Three basic disciplines of Christian theology might be identified by the three principal questions outlined here. A fourth discipline might be formed when these three are brought into a certain relation, while a fifth, though belonging integrally to the first four, might be distinguished by its attention to a particular aspect of Christian witness. Though this is not an exhaustive enumeration of the disciplines and subdisciplines of Christian theology, an account of these five should provide a basic orientation to the whole. It should be noted that, while the disciplines portrayed in the following account bear familiar names and at least some resemblance to existing theological disciplines, there are also significant differences. This does not purport to be a descriptive account. It is, instead, a proposal, whose value might best be gauged not by how well it depicts the present shape and self-understanding of the various disciplines, but by how well it represents the structure and dynamics of authentic theological inquiry. To the extent that it succeeds in that attempt, it may also indicate some ways in which the current understanding and practice of theological study might be usefully modified. If those involved in theological study are able to place their own efforts and concerns in relation to this account, and are helped by it at all to a clearer and more fruitful understanding of the theological enterprise or of particular aspects of it, it will have served its main purpose. The question of the relationship between this account and the present disciplinary structure in theological studies will be taken up again in the following chapter.

The discipline which takes shape around the first of our principal questions may be called *historical theology*. This name has, of course, been assigned to many different enterprises. It has sometimes been used as a synonym for church history, the history of Christianity, or the history of doctrine or of theology. Such usage misleadingly suggests that there is something intrinsically theological about the study of the Christian past. On the other hand, the name has sometimes been chosen explicitly to affirm just that, and to differentiate the study of church history (or at least the proper study of it) from ordinary, secular historical study, on the grounds that the understanding of Christian history demands certain methodological assumptions or principles of a theological sort. The name has also sometimes been applied to several sorts of endeavor which might more properly be termed "theology of history," e.g., interpretations of history from the standpoint of a doctrine of providence, in which particular events or patterns, or human history as a whole, is read in the context of the "history of salvation." There are other uses as well, including, of course, Schleiermacher's adaptation of the term to designate a particular collection of broadly historical studies of Christianity undertaken for a theological purpose. Given this range of meanings, it is important to state clearly and to attempt to justify the particular use made of the term here.

Historical theology is so named in this account because it is the use of the resources and methods of historical study to pursue the theological question of the "Christianness," i.e., the faithfulness to what is normatively Christian, of Christian witness. It is a study of the Christian tradition which seeks to discern what makes Christian witness Christian. It asks by what criteria the "Christianness" of something might be judged, and it asks how such criteria might be applied in various sorts of cases; and it proceeds then to make appropriate judgments and proposals. Both of these questions involve historical inquiry: the first because the pertinent criteria are supplied by historical data, and the second because it is essentially a question about historical continuity— about the possible and actual relationships of elements within a tradition.

That historical data furnish the pertinent criteria is indicated by the fact that the church has always had to appeal to elements of its own past to vindicate the Christian authenticity of its life and message: to "tradition" generally, perhaps, or more specifically to scripture, or to a "rule of faith," or to the witness of the apostles. The church has always understood itself to be under an obligation to hand on faithfully that which it has received, and it has generally recognized the necessity for some sort of critical sifting of what has been mediated historically, to distinguish the authentic tradition from whatever distortions and accretions may also be present in that heritage. Such an appeal to historical data, however it is framed, is inescapable given the historicity of that which Christian witness ultimately intends to represent, and by which it is ultimately normed: Jesus Christ.

Historical theology reflects upon this appeal to history, and makes explicit the questions it involves: First, what in this past may most adequately serve as the criterion or criteria for testing the authenticity or representativeness of Christian witness, its faithfulness to Jesus Christ? And secondly, when may an instance of witness rightly be said to be "in accord" with the criterion or criteria thus identified? How are we actually to understand and assess the "Christianness" of the Christian tradition in its manifold and ever-increasing variety? Historical theology investigates the Christian past so as to inform and enhance contemporary reflection upon the problems of the identity, continuity, unity, and representativeness of Christian witness.

Because of the prominent role the Bible has played in dealing with such questions and problems throughout most of Christian history, it has sometimes been thought that the appropriate discipline to deal with them is not "historical theology," but "biblical theology." (The name, "biblical theology," is often associated with a particular movement or family of movements in Protestant theology, from early Pietism to the mid-twentieth century, rather than with a branch or division of theological study. Here, however, it is to be taken in this latter sense—though the distinction is not altogether sharp, since some of the proponents of "biblical theology" in the first sense intended it as a comprehensive alternative to most or all of the traditional scheme of theological study, while others gave it a more modest scope and role.) In the old Protestant fourfold pattern of theological study, the study of history was certainly not irrelevant to a concern for the faithfulness of the church's witness, but it was in biblical study—an enterprise fundamentally distinct from historical study in method as well as subject matter—that the quest for what is normative was located. Although the questionableness of both of these fundamental distinctions has become more apparent over the years, the disciplinary division of biblical from historical theology has largely been maintained—and with it, the assumption that the former study is the proper locus for the pursuit of the question of what is normatively Christian. But there are at least three good reasons for departing from this custom, and for including the theological study of the Bible within what we are here calling historical theology.

First, and most obviously, the notion of a separate "biblical theology" appears to presuppose an answer to one of the basic questions at issue. It presumes that the Bible is the criterion by which the representativeness of Christian witness is to be judged. But one of the tasks of historical theology is precisely to test that common assumption. The fact that the church has ordinarily given the Bible that status and function (at least in principle) is indisputable. But that the church has acted rightly in doing so, or that the church's previous decisions in this regard—however justifiable in their own time—can and should be affirmed now, is always open to question. Historical theology raises and pursues that question. It naturally includes the study of the Bible and of its use, and of the claims which have been made concerning its authority, interpretation, and function; but it puts this study into the larger context of its search for the standards of authentically Christian witness and for clues as to their application. It does not beg the question of the canon.

Secondly, historical theology allows greater scope than the term "biblical theology" would appear to allow for the pursuit of the second basic question which was identified as belonging to this dimension of theological inquiry: namely, that of the application of whatever criterion or criteria of "Christianness" may be established. When is an act of witness "in accord" with whatever is normative? (Granting, for example, that "scripture" is the criterion of authenticity, there is still the question of how to tell when something is being said or done "scripturally." Quoting the Bible does not necessarily make one's witness biblically warranted, any more than the avoidance of explicit references to scripture would mean that one's witness is "unscriptural." Notwithstanding our craving for simple techniques, things are rarely that simple.) Christian history is, among other things, the record of attempts to deal with this question, in practice as well as in thought. It can be read as a vast and often bewildering assortment of proposals for conducting Christian life and witness "Christianly," that is, with appropriate regard for whatever the standards are taken to be. But what is appropriate regard? Even where there has been rough agreement on the criteria, there has been great divergence in their application. Different circumstances have given rise to vastly different versions of Christianity, whose relationships to one another and to the common sources to which they appeal is often difficult to discern and explain. It is the business of historical theology to study these ways of being Christian, and the ways of construing Christianity which they embody. Historical theology does not attempt simply to identify and interpret the standards of Christian authenticity in isolation from any context; it reflects upon the ways those standards have been appropriated, and upon all the questions raised by the historical particularity and diversity of Christian witness, so as to open up to its full dimensions the question as to when that witness is "truly Christian."

A third reason for preferring "historical theology" is this: the term indicates the basic methodological orientation of this dimension of theological inquiry. Historical theology is grounded in historical study. In its procedures and claims, it is responsible to the standards of critical historical scholarship generally. It finds its conversation-partners among the disciplines of historical study. It is necessarily attentive to whatever movements of thought in the historical fields might bear upon its own subject-matter and interests, and to the issues of historiography and hermeneutics which are of common concern to those who study and interpret the human past. In short, historical theology pursues its theological task *historically*. By contrast, the term "biblical theology" gives no positive indication of the sort of study it designates. The term has sometimes been used deliberately to isolate biblical study from critical historical inquiry, and from other secular disciplines. Even when such isolation is not intended, the use of this term naturally raises some questions about the character and accountability of the discipline so designated. The study of the Bible occupies a prominent place in historical theology, but that prominence does not warrant bestowing upon it a title which obscures its own identity and its relation to its proper context as an historical and theological study.

All of this is not to deny the propriety or usefulness of approaching the Bible—or its component texts, or, indeed, the later Christian tradition—with tools and methods of study other than those supplied by critical historical scholarship. It may well be that an understanding of the normative significance of scripture requires other ways of attending to the text, and that principles derived from sources as wide-ranging as "pre-critical" biblical exegesis and contemporary literary theory may be found illuminating. Perhaps, as some have suggested, the Bible needs to be regarded not as a collection of historical sources but rather as an unconventional novel, or poem, or set of oracles, or in some other way, if its normative bearing on Christian witness is to be realized. Perhaps other segments or elements of Christian tradition can be similarly illuminated by an application of other modes of reading or forms of analysis from those ordinarily associated with historical study. Such strategies can readily be incorporated into historical theology, without violating its character as such. Just as the historical study of seventeenth-century English literature requires a mastery of some modes of literary understanding, or just as the study of the history of economics requires some grasp of economic theory, so historical theology may involve a variety of interpretative techniques and competences. In any case, the choice and use of such alternatives is determined in accord with the aims of the inquiry.

The second of our principal theological questions, that of the truth of Christian witness, is the focus of a second discipline, which may be called *philosophical theology*. Like "historical theology," this term has been applied to a variety of concerns, and has often been used synonymously with such terms as "philosophy of religion" and "natural theology." Occasionally, as with Schleiermacher, it has been applied to a component of Christian theology, but more often it has represented an independent inquiry, unrelated to any particular religious tradition. It is important to indicate what is intended here in using the term to designate a basic discipline of Christian theology.

Just as historical theology is so named because its principal methods are those of historical study, so the adjective "philosophical" here discloses the methodological orientation of this branch of theological inquiry. And just as historical theology is not just another name for the historical study of Christian witness, but is rather the use of historical study for theological purposes, so philosophical theology is not just the philosophical study of that witness. If it were, it might find its proper context within the philosophical study of religion generally. However, in philosophical theology, that philosophical study is put to a theological use.

The philosophical study of any human activity aims at exhibiting the "logic" of that activity, that is, at uncovering the principles relevant to its understanding and criticism. Since human beings tend to talk about what they do, and indeed since talk is often directly involved in the doing, a philosophical study typically involves coming to terms with the

pertinent body of discourse so as to clarify the conditions of meaningful
and appropriate thought and speech with regard to the activity in question. A philosophical study of Christian witness, whether undertaken as
part of the philosophy of religion or (as in Christian theology) under
other auspices, thus aims to discover and display the sorts of meaning
the discourse and activity of Christian witness involve, including the
sorts of claims to truth which that witness may make.

On some accounts of the scope of philosophy, it does not pertain to
philosophical inquiry to move beyond the determination of the criteria
for meaning and truth in a given area of discourse to the making of
actual judgments concerning the meaning or truth of what is said
therein. Such judgments are not properly philosophical, but rather, say,
scientific or historical or aesthetic. Philosophy, on this account, has the
task of clarifying what such judgments involve in a given field, but the
task of making them falls to the users of the discourse whose principles
are thus clarified. (There is, of course, nothing to prevent a philosopher
of science from also making scientific judgments; but in doing so, he or
she is no longer functioning as philosopher, but as scientist.) This delim-
itation of the scope of philosophy is not universally accepted. Few things
in philosophy are. Further, although it has a certain attractive elegance
and is persuasive in some instances, there are some forms of discourse
(including some in which the word "God" is prominent, e.g., versions of
the so-called ontological argument for the existence of God) which
steadfastly resist the categorization it imposes. But whatever may be the
case with philosophy itself, there can be no doubt that philosophical
theology does move beyond the identification of criteria and procedures
for judgment to the making of actual judgments concerning the meaning and truth of Christian witness. It uses the resources of philosophical
inquiry to pursue the critical theological question: Is this witness true?

Both the variety of approaches to philosophy and the complexity and
diversity of Christian witness itself make philosophical theology a multi-
farious enterprise. To identify it as one of the basic theological disciplines is not to endorse any particular philosophical strategy for it, nor to
dismiss the serious and perennial questions which may be conveniently
represented by Tertullian's "What has Athens to do with Jerusalem?" It is
neither to advocate nor to abandon "natural theology" (whatever that
term may mean); that is, a philosophical theologian in this sense of the
term might conceivably be closer to Karl Barth than to Thomas Aquinas
or Charles Hartshorne on the question of the possibility of "natural"
knowledge of God. All these are issues which the discipline of philosophical theology must explore. Not even the name, "philosophical theology,"
is indispensable, however clear its rationale. The task it represents has
sometimes been pursued under other labels, e.g., within systematic or
dogmatic theology, perhaps especially at times when what has gone by

the name of "philosophy" has been under theological suspicion for one reason or another. What is theologically indispensable is the activity itself: the discipline of giving careful, critical attention to the question of the truth of Christian witness.

The question of the fitting enactment of Christian witness is the leading question of a third basic theological discipline, which may be called by the conventional name of *practical theology*.

That name has some disadvantages. It does not indicate as clearly as do the names of the two previous disciplines the sort of inquiry it involves, and the non-theological disciplines to which it is chiefly related. (We can identify "historical inquiry" and "philosophical inquiry," and see how these inform the corresponding theological disciplines; but "practical inquiry" does not evoke the same sorts of associations.) And unfortunately, given our habituation to the familiar theory-practice dichotomy, the term does suggest that this discipline is devoted to "practice" while the others must be devoted to "theory." The questionableness of such a classification is increasingly evident. Each of the theological disciplines is practical in certain important respects—e.g., each involves the acquisition and employment (or practice) of certain abilities, and each is a reflection on the practice of witness, normally with the practical aim of enabling better practice. Each of them—practical theology included—is also theoretical: each requires for its effective pursuit the exercise of *theoria*, i.e., the comprehensive envisioning both of the Christian witness and of the theological task, in their unity and complexity. Whatever may be the fate of the theory-practice distinction in future theology, it is at least clear that the facile division of theological studies into the theoretical and the practical is a serious mistake. We shall return to this issue in the next chapter.

The chief justification for the name, "practical theology," aside from its familiarity, must be this: it calls attention to the fact that Christian witness is a practice, a deliberate, purposeful activity; and it identifies this fact about that witness as the distinctive concern of the discipline which bears this name. Practical theology examines Christian witness as practice, i.e., with respect to its enactment. It asks by what standards this practice is to be judged, and it proceeds to make the relevant judgments concerning past, present, or prospective instances of it.

Christian witness is borne by the actions of Christians and Christian communities, and by their very being *as* Christians and communities. It is both official and unofficial, formal and informal, explicit and implicit, verbal and nonverbal. It is carried by the presence, design, cost, and relation to its neighborhood of a church building, as well as by the sermons preached and liturgies performed therein; by Christians' use of time and money, their participation in politics, and their response to what befalls them, as well as by their verbal affirmations. Verbal witness is itself best regarded as a deed: speaking (or writing) is an activity, which cannot be properly evaluated simply in terms of its content. Practical theology is concerned with—among other things—the practice of Christian speech, or, to use the philosopher J. L. Austin's term, with verbal witness as "speech-act."

In an unfinished chapter of his *Ethics* titled "What is Meant by 'Telling the Truth'?" Dietrich Bonhoeffer explored the activity of truthful speaking with rare insight. In a summary, he wrote: "How can I speak the truth? *a* By perceiving who causes me to speak and what entitles me to speak. *b* By perceiving the place at which I stand. *c* By relating to this context the object about which I am making some assertion."[2] If the tasks of "perceiving who causes me to speak and what entitles me to speak" pertain, as they would appear to, to the disciplines described here as historical and philosophical theology, then the distinctive assignment of practical theology might be positively described as that of enabling those who bear Christian witness to perceive the place at which they stand, and to relate their witness to that context. Practical theology draws upon the resources of those disciplines concerned with the understanding of human culture and behavior—psychology, sociology, anthropology, history, and their various offspring—to inquire about the relationship between the content and intention of Christian witness and its context. With the help of historical and philosophical theology as well, it studies the influence of social and cultural forces upon the shaping of Christian witness as well as upon its reception and effects, and it asks how witness may be most appropriately borne within a given set of circumstances.

Practical theology is not the same as pastoral theology, although the two have often been equated. Pastoral theology involves both more and less than practical theology. On the one hand, as a theological inquiry into the office or function of "pastor" in the church, it involves the historical and philosophical as well as the practical dimension of theological inquiry, as it attempts to give an account of that office or function which is both adequate to the Christian witness as it bears upon this form of church leadership and useful to those who exercise it. On the other hand, because of its specific focus on the pastoral ministry, it does not have the breadth of scope which the discipline of practical theology must have. Practical theology is concerned not only with the pastoral ministry, nor with "church leadership" in any narrow sense, but rather with the enactment of Christian witness in its entirety—that is, with the entire life and activity of the church as the community of witness.

It is well to make this explicit, because it is not uncommon in American seminaries for "practical theology" to function simply as a collective term

---

[2] Dietrich Bonhoeffer, *Ethics*, ed. Eberhard Bethge, tr. Neville Horton Smith (London: Fontana Library, 1964), 370.

for the various specialized disciplines devoted to particular pastoral duties: preaching, administration, the leadership of worship, pastoral care, and so on. (Even when this field of studies includes areas related to non-pastoral leadership, e.g., in religious education, as well, it is commonly organized around a pastoral paradigm.) This association of practical theology with pastoral functions carries a double danger. In the first place, by focusing attention upon the various discrete areas or duties of ministry, it tends to discourage reflection upon pastoral ministry as a whole. The result is often a fairly uncritical appropriation of particular understandings and skills, with little awareness either of their relationship to one another in a coherent practice or of the need to develop a process whereby these understandings and skills might be periodically re-assessed. "Practical theology" in this sense, despite its pastoral orientation, fails even to be pastoral theology.

In the second place, the association of practical theology with pastoral functions tends to promote clericalism: the identification of Christian witness with clerical activities, and of Christian ministry with ordained or professional ministry. More broadly, it promotes a kind of institutionalism: the identification of Christian witness with the maintenance of the religious institution known as the church, with its worship, it socialization of the young, its recruitment of new members, and so on. Even when preaching, education, the care of members, etc., are understood as congregational events or activities, and not as the sole responsibility of the clergy, this institutionalism is difficult to transcend so long as "practical theology" is dominated by these various institutionally-oriented functions. Certainly both pastoral activity and institutional maintenance have a part in Christian witness; but their part is essentially to enable the church to be the community of witness in the world. When practical theology loses sight of the proper scope of Christian witness, it degenerates. If the conventional pastorally-oriented sub-specialties of homiletics, liturgics, and so on are properly to serve the demands of pastoral ministry itself, to say nothing of the general ministry of all Christians, they must be supplemented by sub-disciplines geared to the exploration of the work of the witnessing community in the world; and all must be informed and corrected by a common comprehensive effort to envision the task of Christian witness and to relate that vision to an understanding of the particular situations in which that witness is to be enacted.

Historical theology is more than a study of the history of Christian witness. Philosophical theology is more than a study of its "logic." And practical theology is more than a study of its practice. Each is a critical inquiry with its own distinctive question concerning the validity of Christian witness. Each must identify the criteria and procedures of judgment appropriate to its task. Each builds upon the others, as well as upon the methods and results of the cognate non-theological disciplines, in framing its own approach.

Although three dimensions of theological inquiry may thus be distinguished, and three basic theological disciplines identified, it should be clear that these distinctions are by no means neat. There are, to be sure, three distinct questions. One might, presumably, pursue any one of them without having any interest in the other two. Further, an affirmative answer to the critical version of any one of the questions, with regard to a particular sample of witness, does not in principle entail an affirmative answer to the others. That is, one might conclude that a given statement is both authentically Christian and true, but inappropriate to its circumstances; or that it is true, but does not (or does not adequately) represent the Christian message; or that it might represent that message, if only its factual assumptions were correct. However, as we have seen, even though one might pursue any one of these inquiries without an *interest* in the other two, one may not pursue any of them without becoming involved in at least some aspects of the other two. It is impossible fully to determine the meaning and truth of an utterance or other act apart from a consideration of its origin and intention, on the one hand, and its context, on the other. It is impossible to assess the fitness of a given act of witness, or even to identify the pertinent criteria for such an assessment, without attending to the nature of Christian witness as such as well as to the variety of its historical expressions. And it is impossible to locate the criteria of Christian authenticity in the tradition if one is unprepared to read that tradition as the history of Christian practice, i.e., to see the connections among meaning, use, and context. These three inquiries are interdependent in many ways. That interdependence is also a striking feature of the cognate secular dimensions which correspond to them: neither "history" nor "philosophy" nor "the human sciences" names a single discipline with a single identifiable method; all are vast, unruly, and to some extent undisciplinable fields of inquiry embracing many strategies, and interconnecting and overlapping in various interesting ways.

Systematic theology is the name we might give to a fourth major theological discipline, which is constituted by the effort to integrate these three basic inquiries in a comprehensive and constructive fashion. As was noted earlier, in many accounts of the structure of theology, systematic theology is essentially assigned the task given in the present scheme to philosophical theology; further, it is situated strategically between the historical and the practical disciplines, in a mediating role. It receives the results of historical investigation; reflects upon their content, testing, refining, and ordering it in some appropriate fashion; and transmits the product to the practical field for implementation. Such an understanding rightly indicates the dependence of practical theology upon the other two disciplines, a dependence related to the fact that Christian witness involves a movement from past to present and future, from what was "given" historically to its present reception and its representation in a new situation. To place systematic theology at the midpoint is to acknowledge that theological inquiry centers on this task of mediation between past and future, between what has been received and what is to be done with it.

A problematic feature of such an understanding, however, is that it tends to suggest—even if it does not assert outright—that the flow of traffic among these disciplines is one-way. Systematic theology, though it may try to anticipate the needs of practical theology in the way it shapes the presentation of its material, can remain essentially uninformed by practical theological inquiry on such an account. It is assumed, in effect, that the questions of the authenticity and truth of Christian witness can be settled apart from and prior to a consideration of its relation to its context. It is further assumed, for the most part, that this relation of witness to context is basically one of "application": that practical theology is concerned primarily with techniques for moving from the general to the specific, from "theory" to "practice." But for reasons which shall be explored further in the following chapter, these are highly dubious assumptions. Systematic theology cannot fulfill its own aim if it is performed simply in anticipation of practical theology; it must be informed, methodologically and materially, by practical theological reflection as well as by the other two basic inquiries. For this reason, as well as for the sake of a clearer recognition of the distinctive task of philosophical theology, it is better to avoid the convention of regarding systematic theology as the "middle discipline" and to try instead to show how it is a complex mode of reflection involving all three dimensions of theology. The next chapter will develop this in more detail.

Systematic theology is "systematic" in three senses. First, it integrates the three inquiries already outlined, bringing the resources and insights of each to bear upon each of the others, and coordinating them as aspects of a single inquiry into the validity of Christian witness. Secondly, it is comprehensive in its scope: it deals with the Christian witness in its entirety, and gives attention to its consistency and integrity. Thirdly, it is constructive as well as critical: it attempts to give a positive, coherent answer to the question of what constitutes valid Christian witness.

With regard to the first, integrative sense of "systematic," it might be worth noting that the three component inquiries have rarely been pursued in a well-balanced way. Partly because of the particular gifts and interests of different theologians, partly because of the contexts in which they have worked, one or another of these concerns has dominated their thought. For some, it has been the concern for an authentically Christian

witness. Heresy has then been perceived as the outstanding problem—
the threat of false witness; and "dogmatics," the quest for the purest
possible doctrine, has seemed the natural form for theology to take,
often with a polemical edge. Among modern theologians, Karl Barth is
undoubtedly the outstanding advocate of this understanding. For
others, the main theological issue facing the church has not been heresy,
but unbelief. The concern for a witness which could commend itself as
true, which could overcome both the intellectual prejudices of its hearers
and its own bondage to outmoded forms of thought and expression, has
then become paramount. Systematic theology of a decidedly philosophical cast and an apologetic intention has been written by such theologians
as Schleiermacher and Paul Tillich in an attempt to address this concern.
Still other theologians have been primarily concerned neither with the
problem of heresy within the church nor with that of unbelief outside it,
at least as these have ordinarily been understood, but rather with the
failure of the church to both listen to and address the actual human
situation with its problems. A variety of "contextual" theologies developed in conscious engagement with particular situations, and a growing number of what have sometimes been called "genitive" theologies
(theologies of work, politics, and so forth), may be seen as attempts to
rectify this failure. In contemporary theology, such movements as femi-
nist theology, black theology, and the Latin American theology of libera-
tion have produced some powerful advocates of this concern for a
proper attentiveness to context and to the particularities of human
experience. According to Gustavo Gutiérrez, for example, for the Latin
American context it is not the non-believer, but the "non-person"—the
poor, the exploited, the one whose humanity is denied and violated by
an oppressive social structure—who poses the real theological challenge.[3]

Any given theological effort is likely to stress one or another of the
three dimensions of theology—the question of authenticity, the question
of meaning and truth, the question of responsiveness to context—depending on the abilities, interests, and situation of the theologian or
theologians involved. Naturally, there is a risk of "one-dimensionality":
insofar as the focal question is regarded as *the* question, the others are
likely to be neglected, either unintentionally or by design. Occasionally a
theologian will identify theology with one of its dimensions, and will
contend that a pursuit of either of the other questions is improper if not
impossible. Such a contention is not just a product of short-sightedness
or arrogance, as a rule. It is rooted in an awareness of the tendency of

---

[3] Gustavo Gutiérrez, "Faith as Freedom: Solidarity with the Alienated and Confidence in
the Future," in Francis A. Eigo, ed., *Living with Change, Experience, Faith* (Villanova, PA:
Villanova University Press, 1976), 37.

those engaged in theology to evade or distort certain of its demands as they attempt to satisfy others: to pursue "authenticity" at the expense of "relevance," or vice versa; to misrepresent the gospel in an attempt to make it credible; and so on. It is understandable if some theologians liken this situation to that of a person attempting to serve two masters, and draw the expected conclusion: you must choose one.

The alternative suggested by the account offered here is that the three dimensions of theological inquiry must be so integrated, in clear recognition of their functional interdependence, that their goals are realized together. Rightly understood, they are not competitors. Each can be effectively pursued only in coordination with the others. Each must both be informed by and inform the others. This is not to say that theologians must aim for an ideal balance of concerns. Each person has a particular mix of abilities, and each situation has its own demands. Any given effort at theological reflection is likely to have a particular focal concern, and appropriately so. What is crucial, however, is that the validity and importance of each dimension of theological inquiry should be properly acknowledged, not only in a formal, perfunctory way, but as a working principle, in any theological effort.

Systematic theology is not only integrative in method, but comprehensive in scope. It has a concern for the wholeness and integrity of Christian witness. That concern does not express itself in a frantic attempt to reflect and remark upon everything in the Christian tradition, but rather in an attempt to see and show connections: to understand how various aspects of witness imply one another; to see the relationships among things which may appear disparate; to detect consistencies and inconsistencies; to distinguish what is central from what is peripheral; in short, to see how things hang together. (Wilfred Sellars's description of philosophy as the effort "to understand how things . . . hang together" reflects above all the "systematic" intention of philosophy, as he conceives it.) This systematic concern for wholeness and consistency is sometimes exhibited in the sort of written work ordinarily called "a systematic theology," that is, a statement of and argument for what are taken to be the essentials or principles of valid Christian witness. But "systematic theology" primarily designates a mode of reflection, not its written product; and that mode of reflection is exercised primarily not in some rarefied atmosphere of abstraction, but rather when we attend to the particular, trying to understand it in light of the whole and vice versa.

Finally, to call systematic theology a constructive effort is not to distinguish it in principle from the three basic disciplines which it combines, since each of them has a constructive as well as a critical moment. It is only to stress the role of systematic reflection in framing a coherent answer to the question of what constitutes valid Christian witness; that is, in integrating the constructive moments of the three component inquiries. This task requires more than a simple coordination of three individual responses. It involves an imaginative act of synthesis, a re-envisioning which, in some respects, goes beyond those responses, even though it is still accountable to them. This is the particularly constructive task of systematic reflection.

A fifth major theological discipline must be included in this account, since the question of its relationship to the foregoing disciplines is frequently raised. The essential points may be made rather briefly. Christian *moral theology*, or theological ethics, may be defined as a critical inquiry into the validity of Christian witness concerning human conduct. "Conduct" here is to be understood as inclusive of any sort of activity over which human beings have, or could have, any sort of control, and which is thus subject to moral deliberation—from such large and visible activities as the organization and direction of societies and institutions to such personal, "inner" activity as the formation of attitudes, judgments, and dispositions.

As the definition indicates, moral theology is not a form of theological inquiry distinct from those previously discussed. It is distinctive only in its focus upon a particular aspect of the Christian witness. Concerning that aspect, it raises the same three principal questions which give rise to the disciplines of historical, philosophical, and practical theology, and it has the same concern for a coherent, comprehensive, and constructive understanding which we have identified with systematic theology. It is thus an integral part of each of these disciplines, and it may be pursued simply as such, i.e., in the course of regular inquiry in those disciplines. Nevertheless, its identification and pursuit as a distinct theological discipline is also fully justified, simply as a matter of practical advantage. Given the importance of its focus, the special sorts of questions which the inquiry generates, and the particular resources which must be appropriated in order to deal with these questions, it is entirely reasonable to circumscribe this inquiry as a special area of scholarship, reflection, and teaching, and to recognize sub-specialties within it just as within the other disciplines.

The relationship of moral to practical theology warrants some particular clarification, given the fact that questions having to do with the conduct of Christians are raised in both: moral questions in the first, practical ones in the second. Moral theology is concerned to assess Christian practice (among other human activities) with respect to its quality as human conduct in light of the Christian witness concerning human conduct. Practical theology is concerned to assess Christian practice with respect to its adequacy as fitting enactment of the Christian witness. Each inquiry has some obvious bearing upon the other. A moral assessment of Christian practice, for example, needs to be informed by a grasp of the aims and self-understanding of the practitioners, and an assessment of the fitness of a given act of witness must take into account the moral quality of the action.

This close relationship has sometimes led to attempts to include one of these inquiries within the other. In a few of the older schemes of theological organization, moral theology was treated as a division of practical theology. In the present scheme, at least, this will not do, since moral theology involves all three dimensions of theological inquiry, not just the practical. Is it possible then simply to reverse the terms, and to regard practical theology as a division of moral theology? Because practical theology deals with a form or aspect of Christian conduct, this alternative seems initially plausible. However, as our initial distinction indicated, while moral theology may be concerned with assessing the conduct of Christian witness as *conduct*, practical theology is concerned with assessing it *as witness*. These two aims evoke distinct sets of considerations, overlapping in certain respects but not identical. Although moral and practical theology are closely involved with each other, the interests of each are best guarded by declining any invitation to absorb either into the other.

Theological inquiry in all its forms and aspects is an endeavor of human beings with limited resources and with particular interests and objectives. No scheme for the ordering and conduct of that inquiry can be adequate which pretends otherwise. The foregoing account has attempted to depict the basic structure of Christian theology, understood as a critical inquiry into the validity of Christian witness as such. But how that inquiry is actually to be practiced, i.e., how that structure shapes a process of reflection, remains to be considered.

Chapter IV
Vision and Discernment

The disciplines described in the foregoing account of the structure of theological inquiry have at least one thing in common with the "ghosts" of Schleiermacher's *Brief Outline*: they do not correspond exactly to any actual theological disciplines, past or present, and whether they ever shall have a more tangible existence remains to be seen. We might, at this point, call them *potential* disciplines. Whether they ever become actual disciplines depends on many things: their internal coherence, strength, and viability as inquiries; their relationships to existing disciplines; the pressures and opportunities provided by their institutional contexts; their need for the forms of scholarly organization and support associated ordinarily with disciplines; the interests they serve, and the inquirers they attract; and so forth. Inquiries—even sustained, vigorous, and important ones—do not automatically become disciplines. Nor should they, necessarily. Some inquiries challenge institutionalized disciplinary arrangements, or cross disciplinary boundaries, and gain their importance from so doing; others—as Stephen Toulmin has argued in the case of ethics and of philosophy—are *essentially* "non-disciplinable," in that, for one reason or another, their concerns transcend not only a given disciplinary arrangement, but any conceivable arrangement.[1]

Theological inquiry, as understood in this book, does not depend absolutely upon the existence of a corresponding disciplinary arrangement. It can be conducted, with more or less success, within a great variety of arrangements, each of which may facilitate the inquiry in some respects, and obstruct or distort it in others. A certain tension is likely to exist between any lively inquiry and the disciplinary traditions. In fact, what sort of concrete disciplinary arrangement would best serve the aims of theological inquiry is an open question. Ironically, it appears that certain features of the typical process by which an inquiry becomes a discipline could tend to frustrate those aims from the start, by inhibiting that interaction among the various dimensions of the inquiry which is so

---

[1] Stephen Toulmin, *Human Understanding: The Collective Use and Evolution of Concepts* (Princeton: Princeton University Press, 1972), 378–411. Toulmin understands a "discipline" to comprise "a communal tradition of procedures and techniques for dealing with theoretical or practical problems" (142). This is a sufficiently precise understanding of the term for our purposes in this book.

crucial to its success. Dominick LaCapra, writing of the aims of intellectual history, has observed that "a discipline may constitute itself in part
through reductive readings of its important texts—readings that are
contested by the 'founding' texts themselves in important ways."[2] The
various disciplines of contemporary theological study have not been
innocent of reductive readings of the Christian tradition, unfortunately;
and what is to assure that whatever succeeds them will be less reductive,
more attentive both to the complex demands of the tradition and to the
complexity of the theological task as a whole? For an inquiry to lack a
clear disciplinary identity is not an unmixed curse.

It is, however, an inherently unstable, and therefore risky, situation.
An inquiry without a disciplinary "home," which is simply parasitic upon
one or more disciplinary traditions, is at the mercy of its host disciplines
to a much greater extent than an inquiry which is internally involved in
its key disciplinary traditions. The latter sort of inquiry can participate in
the ongoing process by which healthy disciplines are continually reas-
sessed and revised; it has a voice in the establishing of those disciplinary
norms and procedures to which it holds itself accountable. This is why
some care was taken in the previous chapter not only to describe the
major elements of theological inquiry as disciplines rather than as free-
floating phases of inquiry, but also to show how each of the three basic
theological disciplines is an active participant in, and not simply dependent upon, the corresponding "secular" discipline of history, philosophy,
and the human sciences. This means, for example, that there is an
historical component of theological inquiry; that the theologian who
engages in this component of the inquiry does so as a practicing historian, and not as someone who simply waits in an anteroom for kindly
historians to furnish the appropriate data and interpretations; that it is
incumbent upon any theologian thus engaged actually to *qualify* as an
historian, i.e., to become, through training in the appropriate historical
disciplines, a scholarly peer with those engaged at the same level in
historical research and interpretation; and that, being so qualified, the
historical theologian has both the right and the responsibility to participate with fellow historians in those deliberations concerning the
character and aims of historical inquiry which affect not only historical
theology but historical study generally. It is only in this way that historical theology can fulfill its own mandate. The same holds true, *mutatis
mutandis*, for the philosophical theologian as philosopher, and for the
practical theologian as "human scientist." (There is at present no com-

---

[2] Dominick LaCapra, "Rethinking Intellectual History and Reading Texts," *History and
Theory*, 19 (1980), 271–272. I am indebted to Marilyn Chapin Massey's exemplary work,
Christ Unmasked: The Meaning of The Life of Jesus in German Politics (Chapel Hill: The
University of North Carolina Press, 1983), for calling my attention to this essay.

monly accepted general term for a scholar in the human sciences. But it is well to remember that "historian" and "philosopher" are misleadingly general.) The well-being of theological inquiry in all its complexity really does depend, in the long run, upon the possibility of achieving and maintaining some appropriate disciplinary context for the inquiry, in which these internal relationships to the cognate studies are nourished while at the same time the distinctively theological aspects of theological inquiry are likewise acknowledged and supported.

It is one thing to invent "potential disciplines" in theology, and to describe their ideal relationships to one another and to the corresponding secular disciplines; it is another to relate this ideal structure to the real world of existing theological disciplines. If those potential disciplines are ever to become actual, and to take whatever concrete form they need in order to facilitate theological inquiry, it will only be by a gradual, deliberate process of transformation. The possibilities and the limitations of the existing disciplinary arrangement as a context for theological inquiry must be tested. The potential for change in the direction of fashioning a more suitable context, as well as the strength and importance of various constraints upon such change, must be carefully probed. It is only through engaging in theological inquiry under the conditions of one's present context that this testing and probing can be accomplished, and appropriate adjustments and revisions attempted; and whatever progress is made is likely to be piecemeal, and in the nature of a compromise.[3]

The direction of this process of transformation, in which (if at all) the understanding of theological inquiry proposed here will find a more adequate embodiment, can be anticipated here in a general way by referring to some fairly pervasive features of the disciplinary settlement in which theological study presently takes place. A more focused consideration of the implications of this proposal for theological education will be the subject of the final chapter of this book; what is intended at this point is simply an indication of some of the most striking assets and liabilities of the present situation as a context for theological inquiry. This brief stocktaking will lead to that consideration of the dynamics of theological inquiry which is the main purpose of this chapter.

If Christian theology is rightly regarded as a critical inquiry, as was argued in the second chapter, then the basic movement of the theological disciplines toward greater critical freedom—the movement which has led over the past two centuries or so to their emergence as independent,

---

[3] I agree here with the argument of Joseph C. Hough, Jr., "Reform in Theological Education as a Political Task," *Theological Education*, 17 (1981), 157–159, that progress is more likely to result from a series of small incremental decisions and changes which give impetus to other developments than from a more massive effort to substitute a whole new program for an old one.

"secular" disciplines—has been, for all its difficulties, a movement in the right direction. It has promoted that freedom from tradition upon which a radical faithfulness *to* tradition depends. It has fostered critical reflection upon the Christian tradition with respect to its genuineness, its meaning and truth, and its fitting enactment—those three dimensions of criticism which our third chapter identified as comprising theological inquiry. It has made it abundantly clear that Christian witness, however inspired, is a human activity, subject to human faults and limitations; and that Christians who hide behind the Bible or the security of tradition in order to fend off inconvenient questions are no more responsible stewards of the gospel than patriots who wrap themselves in the flag from similar motives are responsible citizens of their country.

Such critical freedom is not a modern discovery, of course. It has a long and respectable history in the church. At particular times and places, one or another of the basic critical questions has been pursued with special vigor, and with notable results: e.g., the "philosophical" question of meaning and truth at the time of the early apologists, the "historical" question of the authenticity of witness at the time of the Reformation, and the "practical" question of how to live out the gospel during the period of the monastic reforms and revivals of the tenth and twelfth centuries. Criticism was not born with the Enlightenment. What the post-Enlightenment developments have produced are certain traditions of critical inquiry (our modern scholarly disciplines and their antecedents and variants) which embody certain well-tested procedures, and are in turn embodied in institutional contexts and political settings which sustain them.

These developments have not been of unambiguously positive import for theology. This is not because the criticism has gone too far, but rather because it has not always gone far enough. We might broaden Karl Barth's advice to the biblical scholars, and affirm that theologians in general must strive to be *more* critical, not less.[4] The scope of criticism has often been unduly restricted. At times, for example, what might be called "political" constraints, imposed with more or less explicitness by church or state or school, have exempted certain questions or areas from attention, or have limited the depth of an inquiry.[5] When theologians internalize such constraints, from whatever motive, the constraints may function more powerfully than when they are recognized and resented as interference. The ideology of theological inquiry—the ways in which

---

[4] In the Foreword to the second edition of *The Epistle to the Romans;* see the translation by Keith R. Crim in *The Beginnings of Dialectic Theology,* Volume One, ed. James M. Robinson (Richmond: John Knox Press, 1968), 93.

[5] On such influences on the development of modern theological study in Germany, see Robert M. Bigler, *The Politics of German Protestantism: The Rise of the Protestant Church Elite in Prussia. 1815–1848* (Berkeley: University of California Press, 1972).

theologians' social location and social interests may lead them unwittingly both to distort and to misrepresent their inquiry—deserves careful
study; such study is indeed one of the ways in which theology needs to
become "more critical," in this case, self-critical.[6]

Often related to such "ideological" constraints, but worth identifying
on their own, are the limitations imposed by disciplinary arrangements
and their institutional contexts. The separation of "scientific" from
"practical" concerns in the German university tradition, and the consequent devaluation not only of practical theology but also of the practical aspects of the "theoretical" disciplines, had its roots in the German
political and social situation and was sustained by it. It helped to elevate
the prestige of "scientific" knowledge, and of the universities which
cultivated it, in an aristocratic culture which was disdainful of the merely
practical. At the same time, it reassured the civil and ecclesiastical powers
that the liberty of inquiry which scholars sought was no threat to the
established order—that (as Kant was to argue[7]) intellectual liberty in the
"scientific" realm is perfectly compatible with absolute obedience in the
"practical." This separation undoubtedly had much to do with the estab-
lishment of such intellectual freedom as the German academic tradition
has enjoyed, and thus with the growth of critical inquiry. It has also
functioned "ideologically," to keep that critical inquiry within bounds.

Analogous arrangements, responsive to analogous pressures, have
been devised elsewhere, of course. The separation of the "scientific" (or
"theoretical" or "academic" or "classical") from the "practical" theological
disciplines has long been axiomatic in American theological education—
partly a legacy of the German scholarly tradition, and partly a functional
move which, like its German counterpart, has assured that practical
preparation for conventional pastoral ministry will go on, despite the
vagaries of critical theological scholarship and largely untouched by
them. More recently, the separation has been reinforced by the growth
of religious studies programs in American universities, and the consequent shift of much current scholarly study of the Bible, of church
history, of Christian thought, etc., to an explicitly non-theological context
and orientation. This has affected the study of these subjects within the
theological school as well, since it has had an impact on the training of
scholars, the formation of their interests, their understanding of the
scope of their disciplines, their views as to what constitutes significant
scholarship in those disciplines, and so forth. While these changes have
in some respects enhanced the critical study of the Christian tradition,

[6] A clear and helpful sorting out of some principal senses of "ideology" is to be found in
Raymond Geuss, *The Idea of a Critical Theory: Habermas and the Frankfurt School* (Cambridge:
Cambridge University Press, 1981), ch. 1.

[7] Immanuel Kant, "What is Enlightenment?", in *The Philosophy of Kant*, tr. and ed. Carl J.
Friedrich (New York: Modern Library, 1949), 132–139.

they have also made it more difficult for scholars, even those in theological schools, to relate their disciplines to theological inquiry as such: that is, to raise the explicitly theological questions of the authenticity, truth, and fitness of Christian witness which their critical awareness might permit them to pursue, and to undertake, from the standpoint of their own particular competence, the sort of systematic reflection which theological inquiry ultimately requires.[8]

Through both their older and their more recent history, the disciplines associated with theological inquiry have thus acquired some features which have restricted their theological usefulness: the continuing separation of "scientific" from "practical" concerns, and the increasing influence of the religious-studies matrix upon disciplines whose former context and purpose was theological education, have nourished and strengthened an approach to theological study which, in some respects, has long made genuine theological inquiry very difficult to realize. This approach is expressed in and fostered by the typical arrangement of the modern Protestant theological curriculum as sketched in the closing pages of the first chapter. It involves a three-step sequence of studies: historical, "systematic," and practical. Although some courses or components belonging to each sort of study may be encountered at each stage in the curriculum, the typical pattern has been for the historical to dominate the earlier portion of one's study and for the practical to dominate the final part, with systematic theology coming somewhere in between. Systematic theology is generally envisioned as the bridge between the other two. If, as is commonly the case, systematic theology includes both dogmatics and ethics, it is dogmatics which normally takes priority in this role. According to the most prominent textbook in theological encyclopedia in the nineteenth century, that of K. R. Hagenbach, dogmatics "constitutes the center [*Mittelpunkt*] of theology," reflecting on the results of exegetical and historical research in the light of the present and fashioning them into a "scientific whole" [*wissenschaftlichen Ganzen*], "from which in turn the principles of ethics and practical theology are to be derived."[9] Indeed, systematic theology is theology *par excellence.*[10] Substantially the same definition of the role of systematic theology—and, by implication at least, of the roles of the other disciplines—has dominated contemporary theology.[11]

---

[8] For one assessment of the impact of these developments, see George Lindbeck, *University Divinity Schools: A Report on Ecclesiastically Independent Theological Education* (Rockefeller Foundation, 1976), 17–18, 35–41.

[9] K. R. Hagenbach, *Encyklopädie und Methodologie der theologischen Wissenschaften*, 12th ed., ed. Max Reischle (Leipzig: S. Hirzel, 1889), 395.

[10] Hagenbach, *Encyklopädie*, 393.

[11] The definition put forth by G. Gloege, "Systematische Theologie, I: Begriff," *Die Religion in Geschichte und Gegenwart*, 3rd ed., vol. 6 (Tübingen: J. C. B: Mohr [Paul Siebeck], 1962), cols. 583–585, essentially follows Hagenbach.

There is a sense in which this sequence of thought and the corresponding curricular arrangement are eminently reasonable. Historical research, yielding an acquaintance with the substance of the Christian tradition, must obviously precede philosophical ("systematic") reflection upon that tradition, and both should inform one's deliberation as to the shaping of that tradition for the future.[12] No one is likely to deny that practical theology should be thus informed, and that it is well therefore to arrange things so that this sequence of study will be observed. But beneath the self-evident sense of this arrangement some fundamental weaknesses are concealed. The key problem, of course, is that this arrangement does not readily permit practical theology to inform the other two dimensions of study—only to be informed by them. As a principal consequence of this one-sidedness, however, even that latter goal is rendered unattainable: that is, *because* practical theology does not inform the other two, it in turn cannot usefully be informed by them.

The normal idiom in which this outcome is discussed is that of "theory and practice." Whether this idiom does more to illuminate than to obscure the issues is debatable. It tends to perpetuate the conventional dichotomy between so-called "theoretical" (*"wissenschaftlich"*, "academic") and "practical" disciplines, and at the same time to promote a false impression of agreement on terms. In fact, the distinction is applied in several different, partly conflicting ways. There are several versions of "the problem of theory and practice" in theology, and it may be well to identify some of the principal ones.

There is, first, the version stemming from what might be called the classic account of the distinction: *theoria* and *praxis* are *essentially* unrelated. They are two different activities, or modes of life. *Theoria* is knowledge, or knowing, for its own sake; it has no pertinence to *praxis*, to the responsible conduct of life, because the things that *theoria* knows are not the sorts of things that can inform one's deliberations about conduct. (For Aristotle, for instance, the object of theory is the realm of the necessary and changeless, not the realm over which human beings have some control. But one need not dichotomize the *objects* of theoretical and practical understanding in order to distinguish them as ways of knowing.

---

[12] This temporal sequence in theological method is a structural principle of the account offered by Schubert M. Ogden in "What Is Theology?", *The Journal of Religion*, 52 (1972), 22–40, where historical theology inquires as to what the Christian witness has already been, systematic theology as to what it is, and practical theology as to what it should now become. It should be noted, however, that Ogden's account is considerably more complex than some of its predecessors in this vein, particularly in its clear recognition of the interdependence of these disciplines. He specifically acknowledges the role of practical theology in drawing attention to features of the contemporary context which must be respected by historical and systematic theology as well if their statements are to be understandable (34). Such features of Ogden's proposal may be read as a corrective to the common tendency toward a "one-way" progression through the disciplines.

It is their *aims* which distinguish them fundamentally, and which can lead them to "know different things" even concerning the same object.) *Praxis* is to be guided, not by theory, but by "practical wisdom" *(phronesis),* which may attain a more reflective mode as "practical philosophy," but which is in no proper sense theoretical. To complain of theoretical knowledge that it is not practical would be, in terms of this account, simply to reveal one's conceptual confusion, since it is not the aim of theory to be practical.[13]

Given this understanding of "theory," one might see "the problem of theory and practice" in theology as a problem centering in the theoretical disciplines. And the problem with the theoretical disciplines is precisely that they are theoretical disciplines. That is, they are geared toward the production of knowledge, rather than toward the cultivation of practical wisdom. The solution to the problem would then take the form of a transformation of these theoretical disciplines into practical disciplines, insofar as their subject matter has any pertinence to *praxis*— or, what is more likely, a thorough reorientation of the whole structure of theological study to conform with its proper character as practical inquiry. Although the problem centers in the theoretical disciplines, it also affects what is presently called "practical theology" as well, so that the latter cannot simply retain its present self-understanding and procedures but must find a new relationship to the whole. (An alternative reading of the problem, given the same understanding of "theory," might, of course, yield an alternative solution: identifying theology as *properly* a theoretical or "scientific" pursuit, it would excise from the theological curriculum any merely practical studies, perhaps relegating them to pastoral training institutes. This solution, too, has had its advocates.)

A second and perhaps more common version of the problem is produced when "theory" and "practice" are seen not as *essentially,* but rather as accidentally and unfortunately, unrelated. Theoretical knowledge is, or should be, pertinent to practice; deliberation concerning practice requires an understanding of "how things are," and it is this that the so-called theoretical disciplines are meant to produce. The problem is that they do not—or, rather, that the understanding which they do produce is inadequate to inform practice. Theoretical knowledge is not irrelevant *in principle* to practice; its irrelevance is an unfortunate result of its remoteness from the realm of practice. Theorists, in this version of the problem, are like Francis Bacon's "philosophers," who "make imaginary laws for imaginary commonwealths; and their discourses are as the stars,

---

[13] For a helpful treatment of the classical discussion, see Nicholas Lobkowicz, *Theory and Practice: History of a Concept from Aristotle to Marx* (Notre Dame: University of Notre Dame Press, 1967), chs. 1–3.

which give little light because they are so high."[14] Two principal explanations for this inadequacy are current. (Bacon's statement hints at both.) One is that theory operates at too high a level of generalization. The realm of practice is complicated, various, and changing, but theory offers too smooth and simple an account of reality to be useful. It neither reflects reality accurately nor gives helpful guidance for practice in a complex world. The other explanation is that theory deals with the "ideal," not with the actual. It is not informed by empirical reality, but is simply imposed upon it. Theory originates in the realm of thought, not of facts. The thoughts may be good ones, the theory admirable, but the facts are stubborn. Unless theory can somehow be accommodated to the actual situation, it risks being dismissed as unworkable.

Whether the problem is that of the relation of general to specific or that of the relation of the ideal to the actual, the solution is usually conceived to take the form of some kind of mediation: something must intervene between theory and practice, to bridge the gap. The remoteness of theory must be overcome. Perhaps theorists need to get acquainted with the particular situations to which their theories are addressed, so as to learn how to make the theory itself more relevant. Perhaps some mediating principles need to be found—a sort of middle ground between theory and practice. Often, this task of mediation or bridging is assumed to belong to practical theology as such: it is to translate the products of the theoretical disciplines into practical principles.[15]

Yet a third version of the problem should be mentioned. It overlaps in certain ways with the previous two, but has a distinct motive and character. In this version, the problem with theory is neither its aim nor its difficulty of application, but its starting-point. The most prominent theological expressions of this version have not used the theory-practice terminology at all, but are nevertheless pertinent to this context. Their common point is that the knowledge of God must be sought where and as God wishes to be known. The proper path to knowledge of God, and thus the proper form of theology, can be distinguished from another way of thinking—call it "speculation" or "philosophy" or "theory"— which disregards these conditions, typically by disregarding the particular in favor of the universal, or by cultivating "detachment" in place

[14] Quoted by L. C. Knights, *Explorations* (New York: New York University Press, 1964), 115.

[15] Other schemes provide still more mediating steps: for John Macquarrie, it is the task of "applied theology" (a subdivision of systematic theology) to formulate theological principles concerning "the expression of faith in concrete existence"; these principles are then to be forwarded to the collection of more specialized disciplines which comprise "practical theology," where, presumably, a still more concrete form of reflection occurs. John Macquarrie, *Principles of Christian Theology,* 2nd ed. (New York: Charles Scribner's Sons, 1977), 40.

of a proper personal involvement. Martin Luther's distinction between the "theology of the cross" and the "theology of glory" is a classic instance of this type. God can only be known by one who is "under the cross," that is, through a willing participation in suffering which enables one to see God in the cross of Christ. The "theologian of glory," who hates the cross and suffering, cannot know God, and is no true theologian.[16] Blaise Pascal's *Mémoriale*, with its famous "God of Abraham, God of Isaac, God of Jacob, not of philosophers and scholars," represents another instance. More recently, Karl Barth's advocacy of a theology based solely on God's self-revelation in Jesus Christ, disclaiming any "natural" knowledge of God, has carried this theme forward. (Although Barth often took Schleiermacher as his chief opponent at this point, Schleiermacher was equally insistent in his own way that Christian theology must avoid all "speculative" thought and must be rooted in what has been accomplished in Jesus Christ.)

Taking "theory" to stand for what such thinkers have also variously called "speculation" or "philosophy," the problem of theory and practice in theology arises, on this account, from the attempt to guide Christian practice by a form of theology which, whatever it may be, cannot be genuine Christian theology because it is not genuinely derived from a faithful appropriation of God's self-revelation. The further specification of the problem can take different forms, of course, depending on what one understands genuine theology to entail. Its solution—again speaking broadly—is not (as in the second version) to build bridges between theory and practice, but rather (as in the first) to renounce theory, and to find a more appropriate mode of reflection.[17]

These three versions of the problem (undoubtedly there are others) share some themes: theory is commonly characterized as general, remote, detached. It has pretensions of universality; it is disdainful of the particular. It is blind to its own limitations. Its practical value is problematic at best. Undoubtedly much theological work of the past and present, particularly in systematic theology, can fairly be described in such terms. It has become "theory," in just these respects. Why has it done so? Is it because there is some inherent "theoretical" character to these dimensions of theological inquiry? Or is it rather because the disciplinary and curricular arrangements in which the inquiry has been pursued have so distorted its elements as to produce a problem which is not properly

---

[16] See Luther's Heidelberg Disputation (1518), in *Luther: Early Theological Works*, ed. and tr. James Atkinson, Library of Christian Classics, Volume XVI (Philadelphia: Westminster Press, 1962), esp. 290–292.

[17] It is, of course, far from evident that all who use the theory-practice idiom have any clear idea of what they mean by either term. The vagueness and incoherence of common usage compound the difficulties here.

inherent in the inquiry as such—a problem which is, in fact, *misdescribed* as "the problem of theory and practice"? The second suggestion is nearer to the truth. The idiom of "theory and practice" has indeed masked the real character of the problem, and in so doing has compounded it.

The conventional and centuries-old division of the theological disciplines into the theoretical and the practical is seriously misleading. It implicitly denies the properly theoretical aspects of practical theology, and it exaggerates the extent to which the other disciplines are themselves theoretical enterprises. However, the division does not merely misrepresent reality; it also transforms it after its own image. That is, when the division is embodied in patterns of theological inquiry and education, when the disciplinary and curricular structure of theology assumes its validity, it becomes self-fulfilling. Historical and philosophical theology then make no use of the resources which practical theology has to offer to their own tasks. The scope of their inquiries becomes artificially restricted in ways which lead to distorted understanding, and which make it difficult, in turn, for practical theology to appropriate their resources for its own inquiry.

The previous chapter portrayed a structure for theological inquiry intended to facilitate the full interplay of its three primary constituents. In that scheme, the dependence of practical theology upon historical and philosophical theology is certainly acknowledged; but so is their dependence upon it, as well as upon each other. They are not pictured as three steps or stages in a sequence, but as three dimensions, in reciprocal relationship to each other. The interdependence among the three constituent inquiries of theology is already evident in the secular inquiries to which each is related, and becomes more acute as the distinctively theological phase of each is reached. It is time to look more closely at that interdependence. In order to do so, however, it is necessary to describe another relationship, which forms its dynamic context. This is the relationship between two moments or aspects of theological inquiry which we may call "vision" and "discernment." These moments belong to each of the dimensions of the inquiry, and it is in the quest for their realization that the three dimensions find their unity in the mode of reflection here termed "systematic theology."

"Vision" and "discernment" are obviously visual metaphors—the one directly visual, the other by long association—for intellectual activities. "Vision," like its ancient counterpart *theoria*, points to a general, synoptic understanding of some range of data or field of objects: an "overview," a grasp of things in their wholeness and relatedness, a seeing of connections (of "how things hang together," to invoke Sellars once more). When Matthew Arnold wrote of Sophocles that he "saw life steadily and saw it whole," he was, we might say, ascribing to him a particular capacity for vision, and connecting that with his "even-balanced soul."[18] He was able to weave the incidents of life into a pattern, so that they made sense together; things fit into a context for him, and were not just a succession of unaccountable surprises.

"Discernment" (and here there is no Greek equivalent as familiar as in the case of "vision"; *eisthesis*, which occurs occasionally in the New Testament—e.g., Phil. 1:9, Heb. 5:14—bears much of the intended sense), on the other hand, points to insight into particular things or situations in their particularity: If vision sees the totality, discernment is the grasp of the individual; the appreciation of differences; discrimination, rather than synthesis. The Latin *discernere*, originally "to sift," hence "to distinguish," conveys the point of this usage.[19]

Like any metaphors, these are both suggestive and misleading.[20] There are other ways to develop the same distinction. In his well-known essay on Tolstoy, Isaiah Berlin makes a figurative use of a line from the Greek poet Archilocus—"The fox knows many things, but the hedgehog knows one big thing"—to distinguish two kinds of thinkers: Hedgehogs are those who "relate everything to a single coherent vision," while the thinking of foxes is "scattered or diffused, moving on many levels, seizing upon the essence of a vast variety of experiences and objects for what they are in themselves. . . ."[21] We might say that the hedgehog specializes in vision, the fox in discernment. Berlin associates the two forms of thinking with two personality types. In their extreme representatives, at least, he finds a "great chasm" between them. There are also people (like Tolstoy) whose lives are a struggle to relate the two tendencies—a struggle, because the two appear to be in opposition. An inclination toward "vision" invites one to play down individual differences, to

[18] Matthew Arnold, "To a Friend," *The Poems of Matthew Arnold*, ed. Kenneth Allott (New York: Barnes & Noble, 1965), 104–105.

[19] I should perhaps say explicitly that, although it appears to me that "vision" and "discernment" commonly bear the distinct metaphorical senses I have assigned to them here, I am not attempting to establish the distinction etymologically or historically. Each word has many uses, and at times they are synonymous. We will not discover what *theoria* (or any other term) "really means" by investigating its archaic usage.

[20] The most serious disadvantage of these visual metaphors—one for which the following account attempts to compensate—is undoubtedly their tendency to obscure the *critical* character of the intellectual activities they represent. The processes I am designating by these terms are discursive processes of inquiry and judgment, not intuitive acts of "seeing." Occasionally, a practiced judge may make a fairly rapid assessment of a situation or a proposal in an act of judgment which, despite its reflective character, will have something of the nature of perception. At other times, the process leading to a judgment will be more obviously one of investigation, deliberation, and testing. In any case, let it be stressed that in this account vision and discernment are not to be understood as occult powers of intuitive knowledge, but rather as activities of forming and testing judgments through the sorts of critical inquiry described in the preceding chapter.

[21] Isaiah Berlin, *The Hedgehog and the Fox: An Essay on Tolstoy's View of History* (New York: New American Library, 1957), 7–8.

blur distinctions, perhaps to impose harmony where none can be readily found. A tendency for "discernment" leads to a fragmentation of perception and experience, a lack of coherence, a disregard for the relationships among the particulars on which one focuses. The one is a centripetal, the other a centrifugal force, in Berlin's strong image.[22]

Berlin may well be right in associating these two intellectual activities with two psychological tendencies and personality types. Most people can recognize the predominance of one or the other in themselves, and perhaps point to its good or bad effects, learn to exploit it or correct for it, and so forth. The psychological roots and concomitants of the activities are important, and we shall have more to say about them in the next chapter. Here, however, we need to concentrate upon the activities themselves, and upon their role in theological reflection. Theological reflection involves a dialectical relationship between vision and discernment. We need to understand what each involves, how they are related, and how they bring together the three constituent theological inquiries into one.

In Christian theology, the activity metaphorically represented by "vision" is, at its most comprehensive, the quest for a coherent understanding of the Christian witness as a whole. It is this moment of the theological task which is most closely associated with features of what is commonly meant by "theoretical" thinking. In the attempt to frame a general account of Christian witness, the theologian will draw upon whatever resources seem most promising for discovering and explicating its content so as to provide an answer to the complex question of its validity. In each of the constituent inquiries, this "theoretical" moment will be likely to involve the critical appropriation of the resources which the corresponding secular inquiries provide for such envisioning. Insofar as the account sought is one responsive to the question of the truth of Christian witness, for example, the theological effort will be shaped by its encounter with those broad philosophical inquiries which aim, in one way or another, to explore the conditions for such truth-claims as Christian witness appears to wish to advance. In an age of philosophical pluralism such as ours, it is becoming reasonably clear that the task here is not to "vindicate" Christian witness by demonstrating its agreement with some reigning metaphysical scheme which is taken to represent reality. It is, rather, to explore and exhibit the rationality of Christian witness—its ways of meaning, the character and relationships of its various claims to truth, the ways in which it seeks to serve as the context within which all of life might be understood. (Just how the Christian "vision" is best explicated, and with what resources, is—and is likely to remain—an open question.)

---

[22] Berlin, *The Hedgehog and the Fox*, 8.

With respect to the historical-theological question of authenticity, any comprehensive account of Christian witness will need to attempt to make plausible its claim to represent that which is normatively Christian. The task of identifying that norm, as well as the task of establishing the connection between that norm and the proffered account, will require some attention to what might be called theoretical questions of history: Do we really have access to the past? Does it make any sense to speak as if centuries-old events or documents could have normative bearing upon the present? Is there really any unity or coherence to the Christian tradition, or, for that matter, is there a "Christian tradition" at all? Some of the pertinent questions are methodological in nature; others ask for something more like a reading of Christian history as a whole, or for an account of the traditioning process which connects the "norming" with the "normed" and grounds any present claim to authenticity.

We are reasonably familiar with the moment of "vision" in theological reflection, at least so far as the two components just mentioned are concerned. This much corresponds fairly well to what has conventionally been called "systematic theology," i.e., the historical-philosophical endeavor to provide a rational and responsible account of the content of the Christian faith. Recently some have begun to advocate the inclusion of a third factor corresponding to the practical-theological dimension of the present scheme, i.e., the use of social-scientific resources in reflecting upon the content of Christian witness.[23] Their utilization in practical theology itself has become common, but the suggestion that they might have something to contribute to systematic theology is relatively new. It has been prompted in part by a growing recognition that any understanding of the Christian witness, and any account given of it, is in fact conditioned in many ways by social and political circumstances. There are "practical" factors at work in systematic theology, whether or not their presence is acknowledged. When they are unacknowledged, they are likely to function ideologically: that is, the theologian's social circumstances (class, economic status, sex, race, nationality, etc.) will work in ways unknown to the theologian, to shape—and usually to distort—his or her understanding and interpretation of Christian witness. Much the same might be said concerning the theologian's psychological circumstances, insofar as these can be distinguished from the social: personal fears, inhibitions, prejudices, and preoccupations can have a great impact on one's understanding of the gospel. When the character and influence of these factors go undetected, one may be inclined to ascribe to one's own thinking and experience an unwarranted universality. One may also be unaware of the actual effects of one's own version of

[23] See, e.g., Friedrich Mildenberger, *Theorie der Theologie: Enzyklopädie als Methodenlehre* (Stuttgart: Calwer, 1972), 64–71; Robin Gill, *Theology and Social Structure* (London: Mowbrays, 1977).

Christian witness upon the situation or situations to which it may be addressed. The preaching of the gospel, and other forms of Christian witness and activity, have often served particular political and economic interests, e.g., by commending docility rather than opposition in the face of injustice, or by interpreting the existing political and economic arrangements as divinely ordered. Sometimes the preachers have been conscious of the interests thus served, and willing participants in the process; sometimes they have simply been used by others; sometimes all have been relatively oblivious to the social functions of the interpretations of the gospel and the forms of witness being employed. In any case, it is safe to say that there has not always been a positive correlation between the genuine intention of the Christian message and effects which Christian witness has had when it has been directed, with whatever degree of consciousness, by prior social or personal interests.

The theoretical resources of the social sciences and related inquiries can supply materials for a sort of "practical vision" which is greatly needed in theology at this point. They can contribute to an understanding of oneself, one's social context, one's loyalties, etc., which can enable one to detect the presence and influence of the hidden factors shaping one's theological thinking and one's presentation of the Christian witness. Broad theories of personality and of society, as well as more focused studies in certain areas (psychology and sociology of religion, sociology of knowledge, studies of ideology, communications theory, and so forth) may be useful in developing a clearer and more comprehensive vision of the situation in which both theology and witness are to be performed, so that both may be undertaken more deliberately, with greater sensitivity in their context.

Each of the three basic theological disciplines thus has a proper "theoretical" moment, if theoretical thought is understood as the effort to cultivate and exercise vision. Systematic theology brings these three into conversation, in the service of its own integrative task. Without conflating the distinct constitutive questions of each component discipline, systematic theology seeks to discover what light each mode of inquiry may shed upon the others. So far as the theoretical aspect of each is concerned, this means, e.g., asking how social-scientific accounts of human behavior (say, in cultural anthropology) might illuminate historical inquiry, and how both might bear on philosophical questions regarding meaning and truth, in regard to Christian tradition.[24] Each mode of envisioning the tradition—philosophical, historical, and practical—may

[24]On one sort of philosophical use of historical and social-scientific investigation, see Stephen E. Toulmin, "From Logical Analysis to Conceptual History," in *The Legacy of Logical Positivism: Studies in the Philosophy of Science,* ed. Peter Achinstein and Stephen F. Barker (Baltimore: Johns Hopkins Press, 1969), 25–53. Their interplay in theological investigation is exemplified in a work such as George Lindbeck's *The Nature of Doctrine* (Philadelphia: Westminster Press, 1984).

be used to bring out possibilities in the others, and to challenge the tendency in each toward a "reductive reading."

This mutual supplementation and correction at the theoretical level has obvious values. But so long as theology remains at the level of vision, there are inbuilt dangers. Christian witness has an inherent, understandable tendency to articulate itself *as* a "vision," i.e., as a rendering of the ultimate context within which human life and all reality are to be properly understood. In Christ, we are told early on, all things cohere (Col. 1:17); and explicating that coherence has been a persistent major objective of Christian theological inquiry. This is an altogether proper concern and task, but one with inherent risks. Nicholas Lash has pointed to a number of these in a recent essay, relating them to the "self-involving" character of the accounts Christians offer. One is the danger of ideological distortion, as our discourse "will always be shaped and influenced more deeply than we know by the circumstances of its production." A second is the tendency to mistake the particular for the universal, and to ascribe universal validity to our own vision. A third is the risk of misrepresentation involved in the very act of constructing an account, insofar as construction requires us to evaluate and arrange the data. "Unless we construct the narrative, we can make no sense of our temporally ordered existence. But the very fact that the sense has to be 'made,' the narrative constructed, threatens the veracity of the tale." A fourth is the related temptation to gloss over the ambiguity and tragedy of experience, and to offer a more finished account than our situation warrants. (This latter danger may be closest to what Luther saw in the "theology of glory.")[25]

How may these inherent dangers of "vision" be confronted? (It is worth noting that these are essentially the weaknesses commonly attributed to "theory.") What correctives may be offered? The mutual criticism of the three main approaches to vision discussed above—the historical, the philosophical, and the practical—offers one sort. But there is another, namely, the corrective supplied by *discernment*.[26] It is discernment, and not "practice," which is the proper counterpoint to theory or vision in this respect. A one-sided preoccupation with the theory-practice relationship has skewed much thinking about the issues here. *Both* vision and discernment are informed by, and in turn inform, practice, as we shall later see. At the same time, vision and discernment

[25] Nicholas Lash, "Ideology, Metaphor and Analogy," in *The Philosophical Frontiers of Christian Theology: Essays Presented to D. M. MacKinnon*, ed. Brian Hebblethwaite and Stewart Sutherland (Cambridge: Cambridge University Press, 1982), 74–75. A similar list of considerations appears in Thomas H. Groome, *Christian Religious Education: Sharing Our Story and Vision* (New York: Harper & Row, 1980), 194–195.

[26] The two sorts of correctives offered by Nicholas Lash in the essay just cited point in much the same direction: he speaks of the "external correctives" of the social sciences and literary criticism, and the "internal correctives" provided by experiences of suffering and

together—and not vision (or "theory") alone—are constitutive of theological reflection. Theology is not simply "theory"; nor is it "theory and practice" together (except in the sense in which any reflective activity is a practice); it *is* theory (in the "vision" sense) and discernment. Systematic theology, that most "theoretical" of theological disciplines, is no exception here. Indeed, the dialectic of vision and discernment should be exemplified in systematic theology, as its "envisioning" moment is counterbalanced by a "discerning" moment, equally systematic in its approach and intention. How that is we must now explore.

The activity of discernment in theology is the effort to grasp and assess the character of a particular instance of Christian witness—past, present, or prospective. It is the effort to see what is really there in the situation, rather than merely what one has been led to expect. In many ways, it is the opposite of vision: analytic rather than synthetic, individuating rather than generalizing, it must, in a way, resist the demands of vision and insist on giving the particular its voice, even (or perhaps especially) when that voice refuses to harmonize with vision's chorus. Discernment takes practice and effort, in which one tries to overcome the sorts of tendencies in the interpretation of experience which Lash describes.

There is a sort of discernment proper to each dimension of theological inquiry, as in the related secular inquiries. These are not sharply distinct from each other, but tend to supplement each other and even to combine into what we might call "systematic discernment," if we needed a name for it—a multidimensional insight into the particular character of a situation, in which one is attentive to the interplay of various sorts of factors. There is historical discernment, which, rather than viewing each individual character or incident as only an instance of some collectivity or trend, is able to see the specific, the novel, and to appreciate the way even the "typical" diverges from type. In historical theology, such discernment permits one to recognize the peculiar dialectic between continuity and discontinuity in tradition: to recognize, on occasion, the orthodoxy of the radically heterodox, or the faithlessness of apparent orthodoxy. One who cultivates discernment in this regard has the sort of freedom with the resources of the Christian tradition which a fluent speaker of a natural language has with its resources: a freedom to sort through the seeming chaos of possibilities for expression, and to say just what he or she means to say.

It would perhaps be more accurate to say that historical discernment is *one* condition of such fluency. For in order to convey an historically authentic witness, one must also convey it intelligibly and effectively to its recipients. These latter two requirements pose the need for the sorts of discernment proper to the other two theological dimensions. Philosophical discernment involves a keen logical and conceptual discrimination, a sense for differences which can only be developed through painstaking attention to individual cases in all their detail. One must fight the "craving for generality," according to Ludwig Wittgenstein (himself an exemplary practitioner of philosophical discernment, who reportedly once thought of using as a motto for his chief work a line from *King Lear*: "I'll teach you differences!").[27] Wittgenstein stressed the necessity of looking closely at a given concept or statement, and to follow out its use, looking to its implications and effects, in order to determine its meaning. "One cannot guess how a word functions. One has to *look at* its use and learn from that."[28] He repeatedly exhorted: "Don't think, but look!"[29] If philosophical vision is (as Whitehead characterized metaphysics) the search for adequate general notions, or "the endeavour to frame a coherent, logical, necessary system of general ideas in terms of which every element of our experience can be interpreted,"[30] then philosophical discernment is the effort to understand the particular as such, to grasp its specific meaning. In philosophical theology, discernment is the principal corrective to the tyranny of philosophical systems (whether metaphysical, anti-metaphysical, or something else) which would dictate the terms to which Christian witness must conform in order to be meaningful or true. Discernment probes the actual logic of witness, to discover how, in fact, its concepts and assertions do function.

Practical discernment overlaps considerably with the previous two sorts. (It may, indeed, be misleading to distinguish these as "sorts" of discernment at all, if that suggests strong differences among them. Perhaps it would be more accurate to say that discernment in theology involves several closely related skills and abilities, i.e., for making certain kinds of historical, philosophical, and practical discriminations.) Practical discernment requires a sensitivity to the human situation, and the conceptual equipment to appraise particular actions in context, e.g., to distinguish deliberate from inadvertent activity, to identify motives, to anticipate consequences, and generally to detect the practically relevant features of a given situation. There are close connections between practical discernment and what we may call moral discernment: they employ much the same vocabulary in their description and appraisal of actions (and in fact description and appraisal are often identical; to describe an action is often to evaluate it[31]), and they attend to much the same

27 On the "craving for generality," see Ludwig Wittgenstein, *The Blue and Brown Books*, ed. Rush Rhees (Oxford: Basil Blackwell, 1958), 17. On Lear, see M. O'C. Drury, "A Symposium," in *Ludwig Wittgenstein: The Man and His Philosophy*, ed. K. T. Fann (New York: Dell Publishing Co., 1967), 68–69.

28 Ludwig Wittgenstein, *Philosophical Investigations*, 3rd ed., ed. G. E. M. Anscombe and Rush Rhees, tr. G. E. M. Anscombe (New York: Macmillan Company, 1958), 109 (§340).

29 Wittgenstein, *Philosophical Investigations*, 31 (§66).

30 Alfred North Whitehead, *Process and Reality*, ed. David Ray Griffin and Donald W. Sherburne (New York: The Free Press, 1978), 3.

31 See, e.g., A. R. Louch, *Explanation and Human Action* (Berkeley: University of California Press, 1966), 54ff.

features of a situation. Judgment in practical theology involves moral considerations, as was pointed out in the third chapter; and this is nowhere clearer than when it comes to the discerning appraisal of particular acts of witness, whether performed or anticipated. The question, "What shall we do?" (or, "What should have been done?") cannot be answered simply by the invoking of general principles, but requires a reading of the situation in sufficient detail to disclose those particular features—sometimes hidden from view—which make certain choices of response appropriate or inappropriate.

Theological discernment, in each of its dimensions, has the character of what Iris Murdoch (borrowing the term from Simone Weil) called "attention": it consists in "a just and loving gaze directed upon an individual reality," "a patient, loving regard, directed upon a person, a thing, a situation."[32] Such attention—"really *looking*," as Murdoch says (perhaps the visual metaphor is finally inescapable)—is not easily achieved. It takes moral as well as technical effort, as her adjectives (e.g., "just," "loving," "patient") indicate. There are technical capacities involved, of course: the scholarly resources of all three dimensions of theological inquiry must be marshalled and combined if one is to give proper and competent attention to the relevant particulars. But one must also be *disposed* to discern. One must be willing to invest the time and energy required to understand. One must be willing to have one's "pre-understandings" challenged and corrected. One must be able to acknowledge the limitations of one's vision. Such willingness and ability is not a technical accomplishment. It has something to do with the kind of person one is. It is the fruit of a certain personal and moral maturity.

Isaiah Berlin portrayed what we have been calling vision and discernment as opposing tendencies belonging to two types of thinkers, or occasionally at war within one mind. We have seen how they are in fact opposed: one must resist the tendency to generalize in order properly to discern, and one must overcome the "centrifugal" tendency of discernment to focus upon ever finer distinctions in order to perform the act of intellectual synthesis which constitutes vision. However, these two moments of thought are united far more strongly than they are opposed. They require each other at a deeper level than that on which they struggle against each other; and the most complete realization of either comes not at the expense of the other but rather in conjunction with the other's own fuller realization. Berlin is quite possibly correct in depicting how the two may act against each other in any given case, or even in setting up a sort of divide within the human race as a whole so far as our typical habits of thought are concerned. The fact remains that there is no

[32] Iris Murdoch, *The Sovereignty of Good* (New York: Schocken Books, 1971), 34, 40, 91.

vision without discernment, and no discernment without vision. Properly developed and related, these two moments of thought serve each other. Their proper development and relationship is crucial to the success of theological inquiry.

The reliance of discernment on vision is clear when we consider that truth which a number of philosophers, historians, and anthropologists have brought forcefully to our attention: namely, that there are no "bare facts." Our ability to distinguish facts, to sort out the particulars of our experience, depends upon our bringing to that experience some sort of interpretative scheme. Wilfrid Sellars, in an influential essay attacking what he calls "the Myth of the Given," notes that "we now recognize that instead of coming to have a concept of something because we have noticed that sort of thing, to have the ability to notice a sort of thing is already to have the concept of that sort of thing, and cannot account for it."[33] Our ability to discern the elements of our experience is acquired along with language, that is, along with the conceptual resources which provide a way of looking at those elements. That is how we can notice "sorts of things." It is even how we can notice when things do not belong to the sorts with which we are familiar. The strange stands out against a background of the ordinary. Our conceptual scheme enables us to see even that which does not fit it; and once we have identified the strange *as* strange, we can begin to see what it is "like," and finally to see how it is unique. The process by which we come to see an individual reality as such is one of "connecting and disconnecting," to use a phrase of John Wisdom's: it involves noting its relations to other, perhaps superficially dissimilar things, and at the same time distinguishing it from things to which it bears a superficial but misleading resemblance, so that its individual character emerges.[34] Both the relating and the differentiating are important, and both rely, in different ways, on the ability to see connections, i.e., on vision.

The reliance of vision on discernment is perhaps still more obvious. While vision is not merely the sum of particular judgments, it does depend upon them for the data from which it abstracts the elements of its own synthesis. One measure of the adequacy of vision is the extent and quality of its openness to being informed by a wealth of particulars, and transformed as new discernment prompts revision or "re-envisioning" of the whole. Wittgenstein once observed that "a main cause of philosophical disease"—we might say, of diseased vision—is "a one-sided diet: one nourishes one's thinking with only one kind of example."[35] A

[33] Wilfrid Sellars, "Empiricism and the Philosophy of Mind," *Science, Perception and Reality* (London: Routledge & Kegan Paul, 1963), 176.

[34] John Wisdom, "Gods," *Philosophy and Psychoanalysis* (Oxford: Basil Blackwell, 1969), 159–163.

[35] Wittgenstein, *Philosophical Investigations*, 155 (§593).

richer diet of discernment helps to assure healthier vision, that is, vision which is itself richer, more complex, more able to integrate the diversity of experience without imposing a false simplicity upon it. Mastering the complexity of one particular incident or concept may open up new possibilities for understanding others, for seeing connections which had previously been hidden—and perhaps for seeing that some of the connections one had earlier made were misconceived. Discernment and vision serve each other as much by the challenges each poses to the other as by the mutual support they render. Each challenges the other to a more adequate performance of its own task, and in their dialectical relation the capacity for genuine practical judgment is formed.

John Wisdom tells of a keeper at the Dublin zoo who had a record of unusual success at the difficult task of breeding lions. "Asked the secret of his success, Mr. Flood replied, 'Understanding lions.' Asked in what consists the understanding of lions, he replied, 'Every lion is different.' "[36]

[36] John Wisdom, "Paradox and Discovery," *Paradox and Discovery* (Oxford: Basil Blackwell, 1965), 138.

Chapter V
Theological Inquiry and Theological Education

In the previous chapter, the terms "vision" and "discernment" were used primarily to designate intellectual *activities* characteristic of theological inquiry. But it became obvious that the terms also have two other important senses. They can designate the *capacities* for those activities, and they can designate their *products*. Thus we may speak of vision as a personal quality which a person might possess or strive for, meaning by "vision" the capacity to envision; or we may speak of someone's vision of the Christian faith, meaning the general understanding of it which he or she has attained and might articulate for us in a summary account, or perhaps in a multivolume written "systematic theology." We may praise someone's discernment, meaning his or her capacity for insight into particular situations, or we may refer to the discernment which someone has of a particular situation, meaning the actual appraisal of it which that person has made.

In their range of senses, these two terms resemble the more general term, "judgment," of which vision and discernment are both types: "judgment" can refer to the activity of judging, to the capacity to judge, or to the outcome. In Chapter Two, we encountered these three senses in connection with the term "theology," which, as we saw, can designate the activity of theological inquiry (its primary sense), the theological capacity or *habitus* (the so-called subjective sense), or the results of theological inquiry, e.g., theological judgments or proposals (the so-called objective sense).

In its own way, of course, the theological *habitus* is also a product of theological inquiry; that is, the capacity and disposition for theology is developed through active participation in it, just as many other abilities and aptitudes are gained and strengthened through exercise. Theological education is essentially just such a participation in theological inquiry, ordered to the acquisition of that complex set of intellectual and personal qualities which go to make up what we might still call the theological *habitus*.

Keeping in mind these two different sorts of products of theological inquiry, the "objective" and the "subjective," we might, then, distinguish between two uses of theological inquiry. Let us call one its *normal* use, and the other its *educational* use. Its normal use is the attainment of considered judgments concerning Christian witness. One normally engages in theological reflection in order to answer a question concerning that witness. It may be a broad question, e.g., as to what the substance of the Christian witness really is, or it may be a much narrower question, e.g., as to how that witness might be most appropriately enacted in a particular instance. As a rule, such judgments—both the broader and the narrower variety—have implications for action. Christians ordinarily engage in theological reflection for the sake of their own Christian practice; their reflection has a deliberative character.

The educational use of theological inquiry also involves the making of theological judgments, and also has a practical intention; but its more proper aim is not the formation of judgments, but the formation of judgment. Its impact upon Christian practice is indirect. It informs practice by equipping the practitioner not with ready-made deliberative judgments but rather with the capacity to make them. The educational use of theological inquiry, then, is subordinate to its normal use: it is a "practice" whose purpose is to develop an aptitude for the practice of inquiry.

These two uses are not mutually exclusive, of course. As with any enterprise in which increased competence is gained with experience, so in theology one's education continues as one pursues the inquiry, even when education is no longer one's primary intention. Likewise, the theological judgments one makes in the course of attaining a basic theological competence, while they are not the primary aim at that stage, are still significant judgments which may have a profound bearing on one's understanding of the Christian faith, one's practice of Christian witness, and one's conduct of theological inquiry from that point onward. Generally speaking, involvement in theological inquiry always yields both "objective" and "subjective" results. Still, there are times when a person's focus will be primarily on the attainment or sharpening of theological abilities, and times when it will be primarily on finding answers to theological questions.

Identifying the first sort of focus with the "educational" use of theological inquiry may seem an arbitrary restriction, since there is no denying that finding answers to theological questions (here, the "normal" use) has often been regarded as the main purpose of theological education, or at least of the theological part of what we conventionally call "theological education." On this view, one studies theology in seminary in order to figure things out—to arrive at a set of judgments about the substance of the Christian witness which one may then use as a foundation (a "theoretical" foundation, perhaps) for one's subsequent practice of ministry. No doubt some attention must be given to the question of how such judgments are to be made, but the "how" is of less immediate concern than the "what." The important thing is to emerge with "a theology," that is, with an objective understanding of the content of the Christian faith which can serve as the basis for one's preaching, teaching, counseling, etc. From this angle, professional theologians—e.g., one's teachers in seminary—may seem unduly preoccupied with the "how," and unhelpfully insistent on raising questions of method, rather than concentrating on the matter at hand. Their insistence that it is their function to help one learn *how* to think rather than *what* to think may look like evasion; and their refusal to regard preachability as the criterion of good theology may come across as a poor defense for their unwillingness or inability to make their work practically relevant.

Teachers as well as students have sometimes operated on the implicit assumption that the principal aim of theological education is to furnish students with a body of objective knowledge. When "covering the material" is the major objective of a course, or when examinations are designed primarily to test students' familiarity with the material "covered," or when a curriculum is shaped by a similar motivation to expose students to everything they are likely to need to know about in the course of their future employment, one may reasonably suspect that such an assumption is at work, and students can hardly be faulted for coming to share it—or at least for recognizing it and coming to terms with it as a fact of academic life. (The students may also be unable to find much correlation between the mastery of objective knowledge which is expected of them in various courses and the competences they need to acquire for their future employment, and may therefore conclude that theological education is largely a meaningless exercise, a trial to endure on the way to ministry which has little to contribute to preparation for that ministry except perhaps a schooling in patience and the endurance of frustration.)

This prevalent working assumption concerning the aim of theological education is a powerful half-truth. It is not simply mistaken, because certainly one of the proper, desired results of a theological education is an enhanced understanding (in the objective sense) of the Christian witness: a vision, however tentative, of its nature, coherence, and implications, a grasp of general principles relevant to Christian practice, a set of reflective judgments on various significant questions. We would normally, and rightly, regard a person who emerged from a course of theological training with no such understanding as miseducated; it is highly unlikely that a person could develop competence in theological inquiry without forming some theological judgments along the way. One learns to make judgments chiefly by making judgments, and then examining their grounds and implications, reflecting on one's performance, and trying again. Those judgments are admittedly provisional and heuristic, especially at the earlier stages of one's involvement in the practice; but to attempt to suspend judgment altogether is to abstain from participation in the process through which judgment is learned.

It is, however, a mistake to regard the formation of such judgments as the *principal* aim of theological education. Judgments are instead both the means and the by-product of the achievement of that principal aim, i.e., the formation of judgment. Their close association with that aim helps to account for the common tendency to mistake them for it, that is, to think that the acquisition of "a theology" (in the objective sense) is the goal and criterion of a theological education. While the possession of a set of theological judgments *may* indicate theological competence, it is not, by itself, an altogether reliable index, since there are many ways of coming to possess opinions other than through a process of careful, critical reflection. One's theology may be inherited, or accepted on the authority of one's teachers, or collected at random. The pressure of academic or ecclesiastical expectations may force a premature closure to judgments without the reflection which they rightly need, and even without any clear sense of the problem to which a given judgment is supposedly a solution. Judgments adopted under these conditions often lack suppleness and vitality. Since they have been acquired at second-hand rather than formed for oneself, their possessor is apt to have little feeling for the degree of firmness or tentativeness with which they should be held, and may be poorly equipped to engage in that ongoing reappraisal of one's judgments which is one mark of intelligent conduct. And to the extent that they have been prompted more by external pressures than by one's own live interest in the questions to which they are answers, these judgments are likely to have only a ceremonial function. They can be trotted out when an opinion is solicited, but they do not belong to one's own actual deliberations. Thus one might (even sincerely) profess a firm adherence to the doctrines of the Trinity and the Incarnation, after a cursory inspection, without those doctrines ever coming to function as working judgments in one's thought and conduct. It is not the mere possession of "a theology" that is the measure of a theological education; it is rather one's ability to form, revise, and employ theological judgments that counts. Vision and discernment are exhibited in practice.

So far, the thesis that theological education is essentially an engagement in theological inquiry for the purpose of developing and strengthening the capacity for that inquiry has simply been asserted. It has some initial plausibility, to be sure. If theology is properly an activity, then learning theology must, one would suppose, mean learning to engage in that activity, and not (for example) simply becoming acquainted with what its practitioners have done or said. Just as learning tennis means learning to play tennis, and learning architecture means achieving the competence to be an architect, so learning an inquiry such as philosophy or theology means learning to conduct the inquiry, or becoming a competent inquirer. And in most such instances, the principal way to learn is to practice in a context in which the necessary resources are made available, training in the pertinent skills is offered, constructive criticism of one's attempts is provided, and so forth.

But theological education has not always been so understood. In fact, there are three other prominent understandings of the enterprise which might be regarded as alternatives to this one. Each has a substantial history and contemporary presence, and each has a plausible claim to the title. Two of them—the older two—are associated with what the present account has treated as the two secondary senses of the term "theology"— the subjective and the objective; the third, more modern alternative is associated with the post-Schleiermacherian fate of the term. That is, theological education may be seen as a process of "spiritual formation" (to choose one popular designation for this enterprise); it may be regarded as the transmittal of tradition—the teaching and learning of doctrine; or it may be viewed as a course of professional training for the tasks of church leadership. In the first case, the focus is upon the subjectivity of the learner. In the second, it is upon the objective content being learned. In the third, it is upon the functions of ministry. The understanding of theological education which this chapter seeks to commend might best be developed and defended by considering its relationship to each of these alternatives.

Theological education has sometimes been understood to consist essentially in a process of spiritual formation. What the future priests and pastors who are its recipients need most, on this view, is not objective knowledge of the Christian tradition, nor professional skill in the performance of the tasks of leadership—though the relative importance of both of these need not be denied—but rather a thorough self-knowledge and self-possession as Christians. Church leaders need not be "saints," but they need to be persons who truly understand themselves in the light of the gospel, and who are able to nurture a similar self-understanding in others. It is a clear awareness and appropriation of one's own Christian identity—the bringing of one's own life under the judgment and grace of God—which is the fundamental requisite for church leadership. Theological education, then, is essentially a continuation and deepening of the ordinary process of Christian nurture or spiritual formation, in which the resources of the tradition (and perhaps other resources as well, e.g., from contemporary psychology) are brought to bear first upon one's own self-understanding and then—supplemented by more explicitly functional or professional training—upon the task of helping others to appropriate the gospel.

This view of theological education as personal formation is common to both "catholic" and "evangelical" traditions, though the idiom, the understanding of the process, and the means may vary considerably. It has liberal versions, heavily informed in theory and technique by current secular psychologies and philosophies, as well as conservative versions in which the traditional means of grace and the traditional vocabularies and practices of spiritual direction are employed without too much attention (at least of a positive kind) to other resources. To some representatives of both the liberal and the conservative versions, the understanding of theology and of theological education advocated in this book may appear to be quite wide of the mark. From some conservative standpoints, Christian formation and critical inquiry are simply irreconcilable enterprises, and a theological education taking the form of a training in critical inquiry would be destructive of the very cause it professes to serve. From other standpoints within the same basic orientation, the relationship between Christian formation and critical inquiry may be seen as one of mutual irrelevance, if not mutual hostility.

The second chapter touched on the frequently assumed opposition between critical thinking and the state of mind appropriate to faith. Faith, it is said, comes through submission to the revealed Word of God, which in turn involves an acknowledgement of the weakness and deceitfulness of our own understanding. True theological understanding—the theological *habitus* or the *intellectus fidei*—is a divine gift, not a human achievement; it requires a "conversion of the intellect," in which our ordinary ways of thinking are transformed under the impact of a new knowledge of divine things. The insistence of John Gerhard and others that the theological *habitus* is a special gift of God was linked to a recognition that human beings, in their present fallen state, are not naturally inclined to genuine knowledge of God. A disposition for that knowledge has to be created, and contrary inclinations subdued. "All right knowledge of God," wrote John Calvin, "is born of obedience."[1]

Given this situation, critical reflection upon theological matters might well appear to be contrary to the spirit of humility and receptivity which is necessary for any genuine acquaintance with God's word and will. The conviction that faith and critical inquiry are essentially opposed is often rooted in an identification of critical thought with prideful self-assertion. Intellectual humility, on this view, entails the surrender of one's independent judgment; unquestioning acceptance is the intellectual form of a proper self-denial. Indeed, some writers in this tradition have advocated not merely a conversion, but a sacrifice, of the intellect, as a condition for

---

[1] John Calvin, *Institutes of the Christian Religion*, tr. Ford Lewis Battles, Library of Christian Classics, vol. 20 (Philadelphia: Westminster Press, 1960), I, 6, 2 (p. 72). On the relation of understanding, practice, and commitment, see Charles M. Wood, "The Knowledge Born of Obedience," *Anglican Theological Review*, 61 (1979), 331–340.

the reception of divine truth.[2] But one need not think of critical inquiry as intrinsically sinful in order to doubt its theological worth. The point can be made more positively by stressing not the natural corruption of the human mind but rather the necessity of faith to understanding: a critical attitude is inappropriate for the purpose of Christian formation, on this view, because it involves a suspension of commitment—a detached, objective approach—rather than the "engaged" stance necessary to a knowledge of God. Critical distance may be called for in other areas of life; but in theology, at least, understanding follows commitment. Anselm's *Proslogium* is frequently cited in this connection: "For I do not seek to understand that I may believe, but I believe in order to understand. For this also I believe,—that unless I believed, I should not understand."[3] The route to theological understanding, it is said, is not criticism, but faith.

Concerning this alleged opposition between faith and critical inquiry, two things must be said. First, it is clear that theological understanding requires personal engagement. This is nothing unique to theology, as a matter of fact. Understanding in any field presupposes a mastery of the concepts involved, and, if one does not already possess the relevant concepts, this generally requires some appropriate form of training or experience. One must not assume a competence to interpret or to judge whatever one encounters; that competence must first be gained. One must be willing to allow oneself to be affected by that which one wishes to understand: to have one's capacities extended, one's vision enlarged, one's ways of experiencing the world challenged or enriched. If, for example, I want to understand what someone has said about the work of a certain composer, I must know something about music and about its interpretation. Otherwise, although the comments may appear to me to have some sense, I will not be in a position to understand them. ("Mendelssohn is, I suppose, the most untragic of composers," wrote Wittgenstein.[4] If I know more or less what tragedy is, I can make something of that judgment, even if I know nothing of Mendelssohn or of music. But what might it mean to call *music* tragic, or untragic? How is a composer

---

[2] According to the seventeenth-century Lutheran dogmatician Abraham Calov, for example, "it is incumbent upon us to accept the Word of God even if our mind cannot comprehend it at all, even if in our minds we are persuaded that it is false." See Robert D. Preus, *The Theology of Post-Reformation Lutheranism: A Study of Theological Prolegomena* (St. Louis: Concordia Publishing House, 1970), 320–21, where this quotation from Calov appears.

[3] *Proslogium*, ch. 1; in *St. Anselm: Proslogium; Monologium; An Appendix in Behalf of the Fool by Gaunilon; and Cur Deus Homo*, tr. Sidney Norton Deane (La Salle, Illinois: Open Court Publishing Company, 1958), 7.

[4] Ludwig Wittgenstein, *Culture and Value*, ed. G. H. von Wright, tr. Peter Winch (Chicago: University of Chicago Press, 1980), 1e.

"untragic"? I will not understand Wittgenstein's remark until I see how it expresses a musical judgment; and for that, I will need some understanding of music.)

Theology is not unique in demanding personal involvement of its learners. But such involvement is especially crucial here, because so many of the concepts used in Christian witness—"creation," "sin," "grace," "hope," and so forth—are what we might call *existential* concepts, i.e., concepts which are instruments for self-understanding. This may not be *all* that these concepts are. That is, their meaning may not be exhausted by their relevance to the illumination or transformation of selfhood. But, whatever else they may also be, they are "self-involving" in that a grasp of them requires (or, perhaps better: amounts to) a certain capacity to understand *oneself* by them.[5] This is why theological inquiry and theological education may rightly be seen to involve something along the lines of "spiritual formation," whatever one's intention. Some such process of conceptual development is not antithetical to critical theological inquiry, but is in fact a condition for it, since one may not properly criticize what one does not understand.[6]

Unfortunately, however, it is also the case that one may not always recognize one's lack of understanding. I may *think* I am qualified to interpret and criticize Wittgenstein's comments about Mendelssohn—or Paul's statements about the death and resurrection of Jesus Christ—simply because I am able to connect some meaning with their words, and make some sense of what they say. And this leads to the second thing to be said. Not only does critical theological inquiry require "formation," i.e., the acquisition of Christian concepts; this "formation," if it is to be responsible, also requires critical reflection. One must test one's understanding: Have I, for example, really understood what Paul understands Christ's death to mean? I might, of course, simply take someone's word for it, or trust my own hunches. But if I do, I will be in a poor position to justify any claims I may want to advance concerning the rightness of my understanding. And without raising some other self-critical questions, I will be similarly ill-prepared to vouch for its validity in other pertinent respects, or likewise for the validity of any witness I may offer on the basis of that understanding. Critical inquiry, far from being a manifestation of rebellious pride, is itself in this use an act of obedience.

There is a crucial distinction to be noted between questioning God's

[5] For further development of this point, see Charles M. Wood, *The Formation of Christian Understanding: An Essay in Theological Hermeneutics* (Philadelphia: Westminster Press, 1981), ch. 2.

[6] This is not to say, however, that one must become a Christian in order to understand Christian witness. It is not inconceiveable that one could come to learn the sense of Christian witness, and yet refrain from commitment to it. The burden of argument is upon anyone who would dispute a non-Christian's understanding of Christianity simply on the grounds that he or she is not a Christian.

Word, and asking whether something really *is* God's Word; between denying or resisting what one knows to be the truth, and asking whether something is in fact true; and between refusing to act responsibly, and deliberating upon a responsible course of action. The familiar association of a critical spirit with impiety or immorality is made easier by a blurring of these distinctions. Admittedly, raising critical questions can be a way of evading commitment by postponing a decision indefinitely. One can ask questions from the wrong motives, and subvert the true spirit and aims of inquiry as much by a seeming interest in it as by an open hostility to it. But such abuse does not negate, but rather only underscores, the importance of a right use of inquiry in the service of one's commitment. Christian theological inquiry, properly undertaken, is normally an exercise in self-criticism: Is what we propose to proclaim *really* the Christian witness? Is what I want to believe and assert really worthy of belief? Is this contemplated act a fitting witness in this situation, or is the church merely performing an exercise here without attending to the circumstances? It is through participation in such self-critical inquiry, in all the requisite dimensions and phases, that one is truly "formed" in that understanding of faith which constitutes the theological *habitus*.

Theological "formation," then, is something quite different from mere indoctrination or habituation. The theological *habitus* sought is not a "habit" in the popular modern sense, i.e., a thoughtless, repetitive behavior. Being reflective is not a habit, in that sense. If we heard someone described as "habitually self-critical," we would no doubt think of that person as having an unreflective and probably unhealthy tendency to self-denigration. Genuine self-criticism, or critical thinking generally, of the sort we have associated with the theological task, is hardly a matter of habit. It is rather a matter of bringing to conscious scrutiny behavior which might otherwise be governed by habit, or convention, or unconscious motives, or various other factors.

The old concept of *habitus* is considerably broader than our current "habit," however. It combines a sense of "capacity" with a sense of "disposition," as the treatment of wisdom as a *habitus* readily illustrates. Being wise takes more than a yearning to be wise, or a firm resolution to act wisely; a *capacity* for intelligent decision and action is also required. At the same time, that capacity alone does not make one wise, for one may have the capacity and fail to exercise it. We would not say of a person (except in jest) something like "He's very wise—he just never acts like it." "Being wise" entails exhibiting that wisdom fairly consistently in one's conduct; it is a matter of disposition or tendency as well as of ability. Perhaps "aptitude," with its combination of "ability" and "inclination," comes closer now to conveying the sense of *habitus* than does "habit." But it may not yet go far enough.

Being reflective, or being critical, is more like a "character-trait" than like a skill, John Passmore has observed. "To call a person 'critical' is to characterise him, to describe his nature, in a sense in which to describe him, simply, as 'capable of analysing certain kinds of fallacy' is not to describe his nature."[7] Certainly, being critical *involves* skills and abilities of various sorts; it even involves habits (e.g., the habit of following certain routine investigative procedures—once it has been established that these are or may be the pertinent procedures—without having to reconsider each step; or, at a more elementary stage, the habits associated with reading or writing a language). But there is also the matter of disposition. "Being critical" qualifies the self—it is a determinant of the sort of person one is. Conversely, the sort of person one is helps to determine the extent to which one is likely to become critical or reflective. To put it another way: learning to be critical involves a kind of self-formation or self-transformation.

The particular ways of being critical which constitute theological aptitude, that is, the capacity and disposition to make theological judgments, depend in part upon the acquisition of certain skills, techniques, and the like in each of the relevant disciplines. But they cannot be reduced to matters of technique or routine. This is partly because the necessary competence in each dimension or phase of the inquiry requires the acquisition of what Passmore calls "open capacities," in which complete mastery is out of the question because the inquiry continues to develop in ways which cannot always be anticipated and which call for imagination and inventiveness.[8] And it is partly because learning to exercise these capacities—learning theological judgment, learning to discern and to envision—is indeed a kind of personal formation. Iris Murdoch, in describing the capacity she calls "attention," remarks: "It is a *task* to come to see the world as it is."[9] The task to which she refers is a moral one. It involves recognizing and overcoming "the tissue of self-aggrandizing and consoling wishes and dreams which prevents one from seeing what is outside one."[10] It demands patience, humility, and compassion. There are, of course, various ways of describing this task and its requirements. The traditional language of "spiritual formation" provides some resources. As we become increasingly aware of the social and historical dimensions of our ordinary self-deception, such instruments as the so-called "critical theory" of post-Marxist philosophers such as Jürgen Habermas and Karl-Otto Apel, with its analysis of ideology and

[7] John Passmore, *The Philosophy of Teaching* (Cambridge: Harvard University Press, 1980), 168.
[8] Passmore, 40–45.
[9] Iris Murdoch, *The Sovereignty of Good* (New York: Schocken Books, 1971), 91.
[10] Murdoch, 59.

its prescriptions for emancipation, are likely to supply other, complementary resources, or at least to provoke more reflection concerning those dimensions.[11] In any case, it is clear that theological education can be properly regarded as "formation"—so long as certain long-standing misconceptions concerning the relation of "formation" and critical inquiry are removed, and so long as it is remembered that the formation sought is precisely the formation of the *critical* aptitude of theological judgment. There is no reason not to regard such an aptitude as a divinely-bestowed *habitus,* and to describe the path to it as a path of prayer, meditation, and testing, and to associate it closely with that attitude of honest and obedient self-recognition and openness to the truth which the tradition calls "repentance." In fact, there is good reason to do so: namely, to counteract the frequently resurgent false and dangerous characterization of faith and critical inquiry as warring forces, one of which must ultimately vanquish the other.

Concerning the second alternative depiction of theological education mentioned above, i.e., theological education as the faithful transmission of tradition, some of the relevant points have already been made earlier in this chapter in discussing the role of "objective" theology, or theological judgments, in the process of learning theological judgment. It was observed then that theological education involves the making of judgments, i.e., the consideration, criticism, and appropriation (or rejection) of representative samples of Christian tradition, and the acquisition of one's own provisional, yet significant, understanding of the content of the Christian faith. There can be no theological education which is not, in some sense, an encounter with tradition. But, as with the first alternative, there are ways of understanding this process which would bring it into collision with the enterprise of critical inquiry. This second potentially problematic relationship needs attention.

Theological education as a matter of handing on the tradition seems particularly important in some "confessional" branches of the church, where the maintenance of sound doctrine is regarded as the key to faithful and vigorous Christian existence. Some of these branches, of course, may not even have what they would identify as a confession, nor would they necessarily think of themselves as having a high regard for "tradition" as such. They may describe themselves instead as "simple, Bible-believing Christians." But when asked what being a simple Bible-believing Christian amounts to, they may well respond with a remarkably clear and well-defined *regula fidei,* an account of the content of the faith

---

[11] See, e.g., Jürgen Habermas, *The Theory of Communicative Action,* Volume One: *Reason and the Rationalization of Society,* tr. Thomas McCarthy (Boston: Beacon Press, 1984); Karl-Otto Apel, *Toward a Transformation of Philosophy,* tr. Glyn Adey and David Frisby (London: Routledge and Kegan Paul, 1980).

which they consider indispensable in substance, if not in form. Other branches, more explicitly traditional and confessional, may be more straightforwardly concerned for the preservation of a particular denominational heritage and identity (not simply for itself alone, it may be, but for the good of the whole church[12]). In any case, the mastery of the doctrinal substance of the Christian witness is seen as the indispensable center of education for church leadership. This may be exhibited in an emphasis on biblical studies of an expository sort, or on dogmatics, or perhaps on the history of doctrine, or on some combination of the three. The pastor or other church leader whom this education is intended to equip is supposed to be "one who knows"—one who knows the Bible, or knows the doctrine, and who is an authoritative teacher or preacher largely by virtue of this knowledge.

Even apart from such strands of the Christian tradition in which objective tradition figures so prominently in the design of theological education and in the understanding of church leadership, there is scarcely a strand in which it is not given some attention. (And even where it is dominant, it is rarely in sole command. Concerns for "formation" and for professional competence are also usually apparent, in some measure.) In any setting, the question is likely to be raised of the form this "traditioning" should responsibly take, in the context of theological education. That question might best be formulated as a question of the role of *doctrine* in theological education.

"Doctrine," in this usage, refers to what the church teaches. Applied broadly, it covers everything which might be regarded as "church teaching," from the decisions of ecumenical councils to the contents of all of last Sunday's sermons and church school lessons. Here we are concerned with a stricter usage, in which "doctrine" refers only to what a particular church body formally and officially sets out and authorizes as a normative statement of, or guide to, the Christian witness. (What constitutes "formal," "official," and "authoritative" teaching varies, of course, from church body to church body. For some, there are reasonably explicit identifying marks; in others, the very notion of authoritative church teaching is problematic, so that the criteria for whatever functions as such are more difficult to determine.) Doctrines in this stricter sense, though they normally take the form of statements of Christian witness, are not intended to function directly *as* witness so much as to function as *guides* to witness—as standards or principles by which those who have responsibility for the conduct of witness can be directed. They are analogous to the rules of grammar, or to grammatical paradigms, in that, although there are few situations in which a direct recitation of the

---

[12] See e.g., the introduction to Carl Braaten and Robert W. Jenson, eds., *Christian Dogmatics*, Volume I (Philadelphia: Fortress Press, 1984), xviii–xix.

rules or paradigms is called for, a genuine grasp of them will enable one to speak correctly in a great variety of situations.[13]

Theology, understood as a critical inquiry into the validity of Christian witness, often focuses upon doctrines. This centering of attention upon what the church formally teaches has had some unfortunate consequences, in that it has usually meant the relative theological neglect of what the church *does,* and especially of what might be called the ordinary witnessing activity of the church in both word and deed, as distinguished from doctrinal formulations. Theologians as a rule have been much more adept at analyzing, criticizing, and reforming doctrines than at reflecting critically upon the actual performance of witness. The theological preoccupation with doctrine is understandable, given the role doctrine is supposed to have in the direction of witness. Perhaps the problem has not been so much the fact as the nature of this concentration: theology has typically been concerned with the *content,* to the neglect of the *function,* of doctrine. If so, the solution is not to shift the focus from doctrine to some other area, but rather to broaden the focus so as to bring into view the way doctrine actually serves (or fails to serve, or might better serve) as an instrument for the regulation of the church's existence. That is, it is the *practical* dimension of theological reflection upon doctrine which most needs strengthening. And if practical theology is conceived, not as a phase of theology which follows systematic theology (where the concentration on doctrine is most pronounced) and deals with the application of its results, but rather—as this book advocates—as a coordinate dimension of that single inquiry which is Christian theology, and indeed as a constituent part of systematic theology, it may become easier to take its distinctive question as to the functional aptness of doctrines seriously. This is not to say that theology can legitimately restrict its attention to doctrine, leaving the actual practice of witness aside; it is to suggest rather that theological reflection upon the practice of witness will be considerably enhanced if the practical dimension is already engaged at the doctrinal level.

In any case, the encounter with doctrine plays a key role in theological education. It is largely through those paradigms or principles of Christian witness known as "doctrines" that the student has access to the substance of the Christian tradition—that is, to the heritage of earlier judgments and proposals as to what constitutes valid witness—and is able to reflect upon it. But how exactly does that process of critical reflection comport with the enterprise of transmitting "sound doctrine" which some regard as the principal business of theological education, and

---

[13] For a highly original and important treatment of doctrines as rules, see George A. Lindbeck, *The Nature of Doctrine: Religion and Theology in a Postliberal Age* (Philadelphia: Westminster Press, 1984).

which few would regard as an insignificant or dispensable element in preparation for church leadership? One might, of course, view tradition and criticism as antithetical, just as one might so view criticism and "formation." On such a view, critical inquiry requires an emancipation from tradition: it means the freedom to make one's own judgments, rather than to accept what has been handed down. Education as "tradition" is then as incompatible with the spirit and intentions of critical inquiry as education as "formation."

As in the previous case, however, this opposition may be seen to be false. Certainly it is possible to describe, and even to attempt, the traditioning process in such a way as to rule out the possibility of critical engagement with what is received. It then becomes a matter of memorization and drill—ultimately of "habit," in the popular sense. But clearly such an approach, though intended to preserve the tradition from critical erosion, is finally destructive of it. It does not preserve a living tradition, because those who are its recipients have renounced the very activities which can keep a tradition alive—namely, those exercises of judgment and imagination by which it can be cleansed and renewed and fitted to new circumstances. Traditions, like persons, stand in need of repentance; and theological inquiry, when it is a genuine, serious effort, can and should be an instrument of self-criticism for the tradition as well as for the individual. As church theology, it is the church's own self-examination with respect to the adequacy of its attempts to bear the Christian witness. In this inquiry, church doctrines—those principles by which the church intends its ordinary activities to be guided—are themselves interrogated as to their adequacy as guides.

It is through such an interrogation of doctrine, as distinguished from a passive reception of it, that persons come to that mastery of the doctrinal heritage on which the continuity of a living tradition depends. For example, only by understanding how the doctrine of the Trinity represents normative Christian witness concerning the reality of God (assuming that it does) will one be enabled to respond intelligently to proposals for its revision, reconception, or replacement. Only by being able to distinguish what is essential to that doctrine from what belongs merely to the circumstances of its formulation is one in a position to adapt it to new circumstances. Only by seeing what makes it still a fitting principle for the conduct of Christian witness in one's own situation (assuming that it is) will one be able to make apt use of it. Or (to abandon those assumptions for the moment and to entertain their rivals), only if one is able to distinguish normative Christian witness concerning God from the doctrine of the Trinity will one be free to consider alternatives which may have a greater claim to validity in any or every respect. In any case, it is through critical reflection on the doctrinal heritage that we are able to make it our own and to make ourselves its responsible bearers.

An understanding of theological education as an education in critical inquiry is therefore not a rival to an understanding of it as the appropriation of tradition. It is clearly in tension with some more or less self-destructive versions of the latter understanding; but it is just as clearly the key to a more genuine, if more radical, realization of its aims.

As for the third alternative mentioned above—the view of theological education as essentially professional education for the tasks of ministry—its relationship to the understanding proposed here is formally different from the previous two relationships considered. In each of those cases, we found that each of the understandings being compared implied the other: an education in theological inquiry is, in some sense, "formation," and "formation" involves learning to be critical; an education in theological inquiry implies the appropriation of tradition, and any adequate appropriation of tradition involves the use of theological judgment. In this third instance, however, the relationship is not one of mutual implication. Its character might be briefly stated thus: theological education is not necessarily professional education for ministry, but the heart of proper professional education for ministry *is* theological education—meaning by "theological education" an education in theological inquiry. One may properly seek and obtain a theological education without any intention of preparing for church leadership of any sort; but one may not properly prepare for church leadership without acquiring theological competence.

The first half of this proposition might be readily granted by anyone who has not simply identified theological education with professional training for ministry, regarding the former term as merely a quaint holdover from the days when such training did somehow centrally involve something called "theology." That is, if there still is a coherent inquiry by that name—if it is not just a collective term for the group of studies, whatever they may be, which go to make up ministerial education—then presumably it makes sense to call training in that inquiry "theological education," even though that might not be the ordinary usage of the term. It is the second half of the proposition which requires more explication and defense, at least in the typical American Protestant seminary setting where "theology" appears to occupy a relatively small segment of the curriculum, and to be one of its more problematic components besides when one thinks in terms of its relationship to the whole. How can education in theological inquiry be the key to training for church leadership?

Theological education is the cultivation of theological judgment. It is the acquisition of the *habitus* for those activities which in the previous chapter were named "vision" and "discernment": activities such as the imaginative grasp of the Christian witness in its unity, the assessment of one's own distinctive situation as a context for witness, and the testing of actual or potential efforts to convey the gospel. The dynamic and developing character of these activities was stressed in that account. Vision and discernment are not merely routine performances. They require intelligence, sensitivity, imagination, and a readiness to deal with the unforeseen.

It is precisely this *habitus* which is the primary and indispensable qualification for church leadership, if "church leadership" itself means anything more than the routine performance of established functions. Recall Edward Farley's observation on this score: "The more the external tasks themselves are focused on as the one and only *telos* of theological education, the less the minister becomes qualified to carry them out."[14] This is because the tasks of ministry require a judgment which transcends technical mastery. Schleiermacher recognized this clearly when he made the "technical" aspect of theological study dependent upon those disciplines which, in his view, are more pertinent to the development of such judgment, i.e., his philosophical and historical theology, in which one learns to grasp and to compare the essential character and the actual present reality of Christianity as a basis for deliberation upon what is to be done.

But how is such judgment to be formed in the context of the present typical curriculum, and how is its formation related to the more strictly professional aspects of education for ministry? It would help to begin by expanding our view of the place of "theology" in the theological curriculum. This does not mean increasing the number of courses required in systematic theology, or enhancing their prestige somehow. It means, instead, understanding the entire curriculum as really and truly a theological curriculum, that is, as a body of resources ordered to the cultivation in students of an aptitude for theological inquiry. This has implications for the way individual areas and courses are organized and taught: although not every course need be explicitly theological in character, the relationship to theological inquiry of what is learned in each course should be made clear. A course in logic, or Mexican-American history, or the sociology of religion, may have an important role to play in a theological curriculum, or in a particular student's program of studies, if it furnishes concepts, skills, or data which bear upon the cultivation of theological judgment in a manner appropriate to the situation and aims of the school or of the student. Courses in biblical languages, in church history, and in other traditional curricular areas may be similarly "non-theological" in themselves, and yet serve a theological purpose. It should not be imagined, however, that no part of the curriculum outside the realm of systematic theology need be explicitly

---

[14] Edward Farley, *Theologia: the Fragmentation and Unity of Theological Education* (Philadelphia: Fortress Press, 1983), 128 (as previously quoted in Chapter I).

theological. Each dimension of theological inquiry demands abilities which can best be developed through concentrated attention to its distinctive problems and methods, and it is highly unfortunate if theology is left to the so-called theologians, i.e., the systematicians—their colleagues having renounced any theological responsibility. Even under the best of conditions, of course, students must largely fashion their own theological education out of the available material, supplying their own connections and filling the gaps their instructors inevitably leave. But there are curricular arrangements which positively discourage such personal integration. There is a place for repentance in the life of the theological school; and this is one—but by no means the only—point at which some sustained self-examination is surely in order.

One final point needs to be made in connection with the relationship of theological education to professional education for ministry. It was noted in Chapter Three that the conventional equation of practical theology with pastoral theology does a disservice to both. It identifies Christian practice with pastoral practice, and it makes pastoral theology a one-dimensional enterprise in which the treatment of pastoral practice readily turns into a discussion of technique. There is a place for professional training for pastoral ministry, or for other forms of church leadership, within the theological curriculum. But that place is not exclusively within practical theology, nor is it in a sort of non-theological appendix to the curriculum. The specifically professional elements of education for ministry are not simply matters of technique, to be tacked on where convenient. They are rather best seen as *specifications* of the broader theological inquiry. That is, here (in relation, for instance, to one's understanding of the pastoral office as a whole, or to the task of preaching, or of administration) the inquiry into what constitutes valid Christian witness is made specific: what makes (or could make) this office, this sermon, this act, an embodiment of genuine witness? Seeking answers to such questions is an engagement in systematic theological reflection—not in its practical dimension alone. It requires a consideration of the pertinent skills and techniques. Indeed, when the questions are asked—as would normally be the case—in the context of one's own quest for professional identity and ability, the inquiry calls for some degree of mastery of those skills and techniques. But it also transcends the technical, calling for an exercise of theological judgment. How the study of pastoral theology, thus understood (or its counterparts for other forms of church leadership) might best be addressed in a curricular design can only be determined in conjunction with a consideration of a host of other practical issues, whose character is likely to vary considerably from one situation to another.

Index